T0246389

BOTH SIDES

OF THE

FIRE

LINE

Memoir *of a* Transgender Firefighter

BOBBIE SCOPA

CHICAGO
REVIEW
PRESS

Copyright © 2022 by Bobbie Scopa
All rights reserved
Published by Chicago Review Press Incorporated
814 North Franklin Street
Chicago, Illinois 60610
ISBN 978-1-64160-806-0

Library of Congress Control Number: 2022935002

Typesetting: Nord Compo

Printed in the United States of America
5 4 3 2 1

This book is dedicated to my amazing children,
Rebecca and Frank.

CONTENTS

ACKNOWLEDGMENTS

ONE OF THE MOST IMPORTANT lessons I've learned in my life is that you rarely know when you're influencing someone or having an impact on their life. It could be a positive impact or negative impact. You might not know which. It's a lesson it took me years to understand. In my life, I've learned so much from watching others. My parents, my bosses, my coworkers, my friends. I'm not suggesting that my observations of those folks were necessarily all positive, but they definitely offered me an example and a learning opportunity to either emulate or to avoid. It's all learning.

In the same way, I don't know if my friends have any idea just how important they have been in my life. Quite literally, if not for my friends and some family members, I might not be here today. After my divorce and estrangement from my family, I was set adrift, alone. But I was blessed to have friends who cared about me, who loved me, and who were in my corner. Wherever I moved to, I was gifted with a new network of loving friends. They've become like a tether to me, keeping me balanced and anchored.

When I retired, I decided to tell some stories from my forty-five-year career in the fire service. I thought it would be entertaining for the listener as well as full of solid leadership lessons. I wasn't sure how to go about creating a website with recorded stories. John Wake, a man who I've been friends with since we were thirteen-year-old kids, helped me with the technical aspects of setting up BobbieOnFire.com. That effort has been very rewarding and naturally led me to tell "the rest of the story."

The writing of this book is my "rest of the story." John has been involved in nearly every aspect through the process. He provided heartfelt perspective to me along the way. Ann Julsen, another of my friends dating back to the 1970s, provided feedback as I wrote each chapter. John and Ann have been supporting my efforts with encouragement, perspectives, and expertise from the beginning.

My sweet cousin Carla was the first person outside my immediate family whom I told my story to. She's a strong and independent woman who's been an inspiration to me over the years. Her business acumen was so helpful to me as I walked through the minefields of trying to find a publisher.

Janessa Hilliard provided early editorial assistance as well as feedback on my "boomer" perspectives. Her technical assistance and expertise was invaluable.

What about the young trans kids and their parents? I keep them in my thoughts and prayers. My sincere hope is that this story will help those parents be less fearful for their children's futures and more understanding of the difficult path their children are on, through no choice of their own.

Thanks to everyone who's been a part of my life. You're loved and appreciated.

PART I

A LIFE LOST

1

THE DUDE

"Go, go, go!"

The fire burned rapidly uphill toward us, enveloping the brush and trees.

We were running for our lives.

"Run, drop it, leave it!" I screamed at the firefighter near me.

He had fallen behind as we ran up the fire line, dropping some of the medical equipment he was carrying. I watched as he struggled, scrambling, trying to pick it back up.

"Leave it and just run—now!"

I turned around to see what was happening. The fire chased him, coming fast in our direction. Less than a hundred feet away.

"Drop it! Run! Run, now!"

He turned around and saw the fire coming for us. Finally understanding the severity of the moment, he left the equipment and ran with me back up the hill, both of us desperate to find someplace safe.

I was the B-Shift captain at Fire Station 1. We were staffed with three firefighters on a paramedic fire engine company. It had been an ordinary day at Station 1. My crew had worked together for several years, and we had become quite close. It's what you like to see for a firefighting crew. That kind of closeness can help with communications and crew cohesion, which makes everyone safer and more efficient. We anticipated what the others were thinking and were going to do. It also made spending twenty-four-hour shifts together with the same coworkers day after day more enjoyable. Even though I was the captain and their boss, to some degree I felt like these guys were also my brothers. I always enjoyed going to work with my crew. We truly felt like a unit.

Going to work as a firefighter can be good fun. Every shift is the great unknown. You never know what's going to happen from one minute to the next. But it's not all excitement and life-and-death emergencies. Some days you find yourself having to conduct fire prevention inspections. That's where you inspect businesses for things like up-to-date fire extinguishers and blocked fire exits. Other days you're working on a routine project around the station—waiting for, hoping for, anxious for an emergency call. Because that's why we're firefighters: we like going on emergency calls. It's who we are.

Before you think that we're horrible human beings for wanting there to be an emergency—arguably the worst day of someone *else's* life—while on duty, think about a surgeon who trains for years, but only ever gets to take out a splinter from someone's finger. As a professional, the surgeon wants to be on duty when that emergency appendectomy needs to be performed. In the same manner, enthusiastic firefighters don't wish bad news for anyone. But, as I used to half-jokingly say, if someone's house must burn down, please let it happen on B-Shift.

A common trait of firefighters is a short attention span. I don't mean to disparage the firefighting profession, but there is some truth to that statement. If you enjoy knowing on Sunday evening what you're going to be doing at work on Monday, you probably won't enjoy being a firefighter. The thing about being a firefighter is the work is constantly changing. If you don't like responding to a medical call, that's OK. Because as soon as the medical call is over, you may be responding to an auto accident or rescuing someone from a mountainside cliff or helping an elderly homeowner replace the batteries in their smoke detector. It's not for everyone, but for those of us who enjoy the spontaneity of never knowing what's next, the job is a dream.

In 1990 the population of the greater Prescott area where I worked was about fifty thousand people. Those people and their town were protected by a city and a county fire department. Prescott is nestled in a little valley surrounded by high mountain peaks within a national forest. Thirty years later, it's still a beautiful and historic little place tourists flock to in the summer to escape the extreme heat down in Phoenix. It was a great place to live and raise a young family. We had a good life in Prescott. Constant and steady and a safe place for my children.

In June 1990 it was going to be hot for the next couple of days in the high country of Arizona. Temperatures were predicted to be in the high 90s. As a matter of fact, in Phoenix on June 26, the high temperature hit 122 degrees Fahrenheit. It had been a warm, rain-barren spring, and the vegetation was already dry as a bone around the Arizona high country. We were expecting that any fire ignition in northern Arizona could possibly result in a large wildfire. We were trained for wildfires as well as structure fires, since there was always an elevated threat of wildfire in our community.

I had started my firefighting career sixteen years earlier as a wildland firefighter working for the United States Forest Service. I switched from full-time wildland firefighting to the career fire department—a typical career transition for many in our profession. Fire departments typically offer better pay, better hours, and better benefits than the wildland fire agencies. So, like hundreds of firefighters across the country every year, I made the move.

Because of my experience at the time, I held the highest wildland fire qualifications in my fire department. When the state of Arizona needed someone to assist in managing some of their larger fires, I often got the call to come help. So it wasn't a surprise when I got a call from dispatch that the US Forest Service was requesting assistance for a fire that had broken out the day before, about one hundred miles away.

I was asked to be the strike team leader in charge of five fire engines and a large water tender carrying thirty-five hundred gallons of water supply from various fire departments from the Phoenix and Prescott areas and proceed to the "Dude Fire" near Payson. Wildfires are named after a local geographic feature, and in this case the fire started near Dude Creek. I was to be briefed when I arrived and given our strike team's assignment. I was told that I would be in charge of structure protection of the Bonita Creek subdivision near the Dude Fire. The

assignment held a twinge of nostalgia for me, since while I was growing up my family had built a cabin in Bonita Creek and had only sold
it a few years earlier.

Responding to a developing wildfire many miles from home isn't
like responding to an emergency in your jurisdiction. It takes time to
put together the crews, since you often need to move personnel around
to provide coverage at the fire department while the crew is going to
be gone. That means you're making phone calls to bring people in to
work who are on days off or shifting people around from one station
to another. It took a few hours before we were ready to make the two-
hour drive to Payson. There were three pieces of equipment from my
fire department: one fire engine, the water tender, and the command
rig (an SUV) that I drove.

On Monday, June 25, Arizona Strike Team One assembled at the
US Forest Service Payson Ranger Station around 5:00 PM to be briefed
and to figure out who was who. This would be the first time many of
us had ever met. While the crews were figuring out radio frequencies
and what equipment we all had, I was briefed by the type 2 incident
management team planning section chief and operations section chief.
I was sent alone to reconnoiter the Bonita Creek subdivision and come
up with a plan to protect it. At this time the fire was still small, and
the prevailing opinion was that the fire would never make it down off
the mountain into Bonita Creek.

Those conversations would haunt me for years.

Bonita Creek subdivision was a remote community comprised of
about fifty-five homes surrounded by national forest. It sat at the base
of the Mogollon Rim, a unique geographic feature that rises nearly two
thousand feet and stretches across the state from northwest to eastern
Arizona. There were only two families who lived in Bonita Creek year-
round. The remaining homes were used primarily in the summertime
by families escaping the Phoenix heat. The subdivision enjoyed beautiful vistas with large ponderosa pines and thick oak brush. That natural
vegetation, although beautiful, would prove fatal in a few hours.

By 11:00 PM I finished driving around the subdivision and had
written my plan for protecting the homes, debriefed with the incident

management team, and was heading back to Bonita Creek to meet up with my strike team. It was probably after midnight before we started working to implement the plan to protect the homes from the Dude Fire. After some fits and starts and amending the plan, we worked through the night: developing a good water supply, laying out fire hoses, and getting ready for a potential future firefight.

In the light of day everything always looks different. Fires that seem so huge at night suddenly shrink by half. We used to make a joke when someone gave a fire "size-up" report on a wildfire at night. After they gave the estimated acres, we'd say, "Are those night acres or day acres?"

It was the same thing at the Dude Fire. When the sun came up the next morning, the fire seemed less dangerous, smaller, and more benign. But protecting the subdivision was going to be a challenge. Even though I grew up hiking, hunting, and playing around Bonita Creek, in the morning daylight and with the trained eyes of an experienced firefighter, my estimate of what was necessary to protect these homes started to change.

Wildland firefighters refer to the vegetation that has the potential to burn as "fuel." That special tree or flowering bush you planted is just considered fuel to the firefighters. That new deck you put on the front of your home? It's just more fuel. And in the Bonita Creek subdivision there was a tremendous amount of fuel.

The natural vegetation consisted of an understory of eight-foot-tall manzanita brush and five-foot-tall turbinella oak. Both of those species are extremely flammable. They burn with the intensity of gasoline in part because they have heavy concentrations of volatile oils within their leaves. Over this shrub component was a dense stand of ponderosa pine. We all knew from a theoretical perspective that this combination could be deadly, but for most of us in 1990, we hadn't yet seen a deadly conflagration from this fuel type in Arizona.

Imagine now that within this extremely flammable natural vegetation of manzanita, oak brush, and ponderosa pine, we plopped down fifty-five homes and outbuildings. Almost every building was a wood-frame structure with wood siding and wood decks. As is common with many remote vacation homes, there were piles of firewood and building materials stacked up against the homes and under the decks. Many vacationers love having the trees and brush growing right up against their home because of the ambience it provides. Even though I had seen the subdivision many times in my life, I had never seen it through the eyes of someone assigned to protect it from a wildfire. When the sun came up Tuesday morning, I felt an unease that I couldn't quite put my finger on.

Before 2001 it was common to work for twenty-four or more hours straight on a wildfire. After the tragic Thirtymile Fire that burned in Washington State, where four young wildland firefighters were killed, it was determined that fatigue leads to poor decision-making. But on the Dude Fire, we had all come to work Monday morning, were dispatched Monday afternoon, worked all Monday night, and went straight to work, fighting fire Tuesday morning.

All night long the Dude Fire had slowly crept downhill, inching toward the subdivision. By morning at the north side of the division, a fire line had been constructed using a bulldozer and twenty-person crews of trained, elite firefighters known as "hotshots." During the night, hotshot crews were conducting burn-out operations with the intent of keeping the main part of the wildfire from threatening or burning the homes. My firefighters from the engine strike team had laid thousands of feet of fire hose to protect the homes and were actively extinguishing hotspots and spot fires. In addition, they were moving flammable materials away from the homes and clearing brush and trees in an attempt make the homes safer.

Early in the day, a firefighter I knew from another department called me on the radio. He was leading a twenty-person inmate firefighting crew down below the subdivision. Inmate fire crews are made up of incarcerated people who attend a forty-hour training program before serving as firefighters and their paid firefighter supervisors. The inmates volunteer to be on the crew and often take great pride in being as good as any regular wildland firefighting crew.

My colleague in the other department had been having radio problems since his arrival on Tuesday and had not spoken to his supervisor yet. This was an unnervingly concerning situation. He had no communications with his supervisor, didn't know who his supervisor was, and had no communications with anyone on the fire other than me. He was an adjoining force to me. He didn't work for me—and I hadn't actually seen him either. But I knew where he was. I was apprehensive for him and his crew, but I was also busy dealing with my own personnel and their safety.

During the day, the smoke became so impenetrably thick that no one on the fire area where we were working could see the main fire. We knew it was up the hill from us, but we couldn't see it. We couldn't see the smoke column either. Being able to see the smoke column offers helpful, crucial information on scene. It can tell you how the fire is burning, the kinds of materials burning, and how intensely the fire is burning, among other things. All we could see was a haze of smoke all around us. It was also hot. Very hot. High temperatures cause fires to burn more intensely, spread faster, and are more difficult to control. In addition, the heat takes a physical toll on the firefighters. To add to the limited visibility, we hadn't had any sleep in thirty hours or so. My brain was as clear as the air I was breathing.

The firefighter working with the inmate crew down below the subdivision called me asking for support from my firefighters. He reported getting spot fires across the fire line in his area. Spot fires are small new fires that ignite when burning embers fall out of the sky and onto the unburned side of the fire line. Spot fires are common, but potentially very dangerous if they are not extinguished. Spot fires not quickly snuffed out will grow, becoming part of the main wildfire. It is a dangerous way wildfire can spread. It was imperative I send some of my firefighters down the line to assist the inmate crew working below us.

I hiked down the fire line to meet up with the inmate crew to see what was going on. The fire line in this location was an old trail that had been cleared by the firefighters and a small bulldozer. It was about six feet wide and was cleared all the way down to the dirt.

But what I saw caused me great concern.

They were in what I believed to be a very dangerous location. The fuels were thick on both sides of the fire line, making the line a challenge to hold on to. A previous burn-out operation meant to stop the fire spread was not successful, so instead of having a safe fire line devoid of fuel on one side, the entire area was primed and ready to reburn.

I knew I should have said something to my friend responsible for the inmate crew. His crew was not in a safe place, and I knew it. I should have grabbed him by the shirt collar and told him to get his crew out of there. I should have, but I didn't. He wasn't working for me, and I didn't want to appear too aggressive or pushy. I quickly moved my firefighters into the area with fire hoses from our fire engines with a water supply to begin assisting the inmate crew with the spot fires.

I hiked back up to the subdivision and spoke with the operations chief on the radio to let him know what was going on. I had no idea that shortly after, my world, and the world of everyone around me, was about to change in a terrible way.

Meanwhile, a public affairs officer arrived from the incident command post with three or four members of the press. They wanted to see what was happening at the fire, but no one anticipated the fire blowing up as it had this afternoon. So now, working on an active, growing fire with no sleep, I had cameras and microphones in my face.

"Strike Team One, Tender 51." That was Rick, one of my regular employees from home on the water tender assigned to my strike team. "Strike Team One, I'm heading out of Bonita Creek to get water, but there is fire between me and you. Your access is cut off, I repeat, your access is cut off."

I was confused. How could there be fire between me and Rick? The Dude Fire was north of my location, Rick and the water tender were south of me. It made no sense. Rick was in the direction of our escape route, a previously identified route we'd use to escape the fire if things turned ugly.

How could the fire be behind me? "Tender 51, Strike Team One, repeat your message," I said.

Rick repeated the same message once again. It sounded like we were surrounded by fire. Rick called back and said he was going to try to get out of the subdivision with the water tender. I told him to head to Tonto Village, a small community within the forest about twenty miles east, where he should be well out of danger.

Now that Rick and the water tender were on their way to safety, I had to pay attention to the fifteen firefighters on my strike team. But before I could call them on the radio, it started crackling with multiple reports of the fire blowing up in locations a mile or more from where I knew the fire to be.

I felt disoriented.

How could the fire have blown up so quickly and be all around us without me even knowing it was happening? I immediately called all my firefighters on the radio in order to get them back up to the subdivision from the canyon where they were assisting the inmate crew. I gave the order with all the urgency in my voice without yelling. I hate yelling on the fireground. Yelling only adds to the confusion and fear in an emergency.

So, in my best calm but confident voice, I said, "Engine 57, Strike Team One. Get back up to the subdivision *now*. Get everyone, including all our personnel from the strike team, with you and as fast as you can get back to the subdivision—now!"

My engine crews started the hike back up the fire line to the subdivision. I began counting firefighters to account for everyone once they were back. Everyone on Strike Team One, including Rick on the water tender, was accounted for. In the meantime, my friend with the inmate crew called me on the radio.

"Strike Team One, Perryville."

"Perryville, Strike Team One," I answered.

"Perryville is deploying shelters."

Fire shelters are the aluminum tents firefighters carry with them as a last chance to get into and escape being burned by oncoming flames. But their utility is limited. I was numb as I heard the Perryville leader call out, "I have one, two, three, four . . ." he continued one by one.

"Ten shelters deployed."

Ten of his twenty firefighters had deployed their shelters. Those ten firefighters were at great risk. Firefighters sometimes died inside their fire shelters; it was no guarantee of safety. And when it is over 1,000 degrees Fahrenheit right outside the fire shelter, the environment inside the shelter is not going to be survivable.

He didn't say where the other half of his crew was. Once inside a fire shelter, your radio doesn't work. You won't be able to talk to anyone.

If you try to lift the edge of the fire shelter up to use the radio, you'll be blasted with super-heated gases, and smoke will fill your shelter. There's just no communication once you deploy.

Now all I knew was that ten firefighters had no choice but to get into their shelters and ride out blowtorch conditions in something fire-fighters sometimes call a "shake and bake." My job now was to notify the operations, or "ops," chief and get my folks out of danger.

"Operations, Strike Team One. Operations, Strike Team One."

"Go ahead, Strike Team One," came the response.

"Perryville is deploying shelters. They have ten firefighters in shelters that I know of. Also, our access is cut off out of the subdivision, so I'm taking my folks up the line to find a safety zone."

Ops affirmed my message. Now I had to figure out what to do and where to go next. Our fire engines were worthless now. There wasn't enough water in the fire engines to put out the fire, and they would not transport us through the flames to safety. We were surrounded by heavy brush, tall pine trees, and lots of homes. The country was steep, so access wouldn't be easy, but there were a half-dozen hotshot crews working in the area as well so we wouldn't be alone.

Around a wildland fire, the safest place you can be is in the burned area after the vegetation has already been consumed by the fire. You might think this is counterintuitive but consider this: If you run away from the fire into unburned vegetation, the fire could overtake you and you'd perish. But if you can make it through the fire and into an area where the fire has already consumed all the fuel, although it would be almost unbearably hot and smoky, you might survive.

Decisions must be made quickly, often with insufficient information. But that day on the north end of Bonita Creek subdivision there was a brain trust of knowledgeable firefighters. The hotshot crew leaders were experienced and would have known what to do purely by instinct.

Suddenly, my radio crackled. "Strike Team One, Zigzag."

Zigzag was a hotshot crew led by Paul Gleason, who would later become famous in the national wildland firefighting community.

"Strike Team One, Zigzag, we have a burned firefighter at our location, and we're going to need medical assistance for him."

"Copy Zigzag, we'll be en route ASAP."

This radio message was just one more unbelievable bit of radio traffic. If there was one burned firefighter, it's likely there were more. Or worse. Everything was moving so quickly, and with literal life-and-death urgency. If I had been any less experienced, I might not have been able to keep everything straight—let alone keep a calm head for my crew. One of my firefighters was driving for his life in the water tender truck to get away from the fire. A public affairs officer with members of the press showed up during the middle of a major wildfire blowup, watching—and recording—our every move. We needed to determine where to escape to in order to survive the fire, since our old route had been consumed by flames and there were about 120 or more firefighters all needing a place to safely ride out the fire. And now I needed to lead a rescue effort to save a burned firefighter back down the canyon we'd just been evacuating everyone from—and there were no other middle-level fire leaders in the area other than me.

The pressure was on.

I gathered up the engine crew from one of the Phoenix-area engines and asked them if they were willing to go back down with me to rescue a burned firefighter. They were not just willing. I had to slow them down long enough to brief them on the risks and possible contingencies.

All I could do was give the remaining four engine crews who were working for me their orders: "Follow the hotshot crews, stick with hotshot crews, and you'll be safe."

It was the best I could do.

I didn't know where a safety zone was, and I didn't have an escape route, but I knew the hotshot crew leaders were experts and would find a way to keep their crews safe. With that bit of minimal advice, I led the one engine crew back down the drainage toward the burned firefighter.

By this time, it was quite obvious we were in the middle of a major blowup. Everything was on fire all around us. But it was like there was a cloud of protection where we walked. The forest was burning north of us, south of us, and west of us, but not yet to our east and not right where we walked.

We made the hike down the canyon until we ran into the Zigzag crew. There laid the burned firefighter. His skin was gray, and he was suffering from severe burns to much of his body. He had come from the inmate crew. He was alive but in grave danger. Paul, the leader of Zigzag, was standing there in a bit of shock with his twenty-person hotshot crew.

Our cloud of protection had been an immense help, but it was not going to last much longer.

I directed Paul to get his crew up the line and tie in with the rest of my strike team and the other hotshot crews. It took me raising my voice to get his attention, and for his crew to get up the line. Paul stayed to help extricate the patient with us.

My medic firefighters began to treat the burned firefighter as if this were a normal accident or medical scene. But this was no normal EMS scene. There would be no time for the processes we are used to when treating a patient. I kept my eyes on the surrounding fire while the firefighters began their treatment. They put the patient on oxygen and started an IV. I told them to load him on the backboard and go—but they weren't ready to load him up yet. They wanted to do more treatment, like they would if they were in their city on a normal medical call. I had to repeat myself several times while raising my voice, all the while watching the fire making runs through the trees and brush toward us. Each run seemed to peter out right before reaching our location, but I knew this luck or divine providence wasn't going to last much longer.

"Now! NOW. Let's go, let's go, let's go!"

Those were my words as I broke my rule of no yelling on the fireground. This was serious. As I suspected, homes were burning and people were dying while we were in the middle of the blowup—not even aware of everything going on.

The patient was loaded on a backboard, and four firefighters, including Paul, were carrying him back uphill toward the subdivision. Another firefighter and I carried all the medical equipment, following the others, with the patient ahead of us. I made sure to be the last person of our rescue group to ensure everyone was out safely.

As we ran up the fire line toward the subdivision, the other firefighter dropped one of the medical packs. I ran past him but stopped to look back, making sure he was coming. I watched as the fire was making a run through the brush and trees uphill in our direction. It was piercingly bright, like a camera lens being overwhelmed by brightness. He was a silhouette of black, the orange of the flames behind him. They were overtaking us quickly.

He was unaware of how close the flames were getting while he struggled to get the medical pack straps over his shoulder. As he pulled up one pack, the pack on his other shoulder would fall off, and he'd try again to get all the gear on his shoulders. The noise of the fire was so great that normal conversation wasn't possible. I yelled at him to just "come on!"

In desperation I became insistent, louder.

"Now—NOW! Let's go! Leave it—*leave it!*"

He glanced back over his shoulder and finally grasped that we were all in peril. He dropped the LifePak 5 on the ground and ran up the hill toward the subdivision.

We arrived at the subdivision to discover the forest was on fire all around us—including where we had just come from. My other firefighters from the strike team, as well as all the other hotshot crews, were nowhere to be seen. I knew they had moved uphill and into the fire, looking for that safe, burned-out area where we'd wait for the fire to run its course and die down. We had just run up the fire line carrying a severely burned patient and multiple packs of medical gear along with our own heavy firefighting gear. We needed to rest for a few minutes and catch our breath.

I directed our group to get behind a home. Using a home as protection from the radiant heat of a wildfire is standard practice now, but it's a last-ditch effort. If your only hope is to get behind a house for protection, things aren't looking good. But we were happy to get a short reprieve from the heat behind that house.

While I spoke to the hotshot crews on the radio to determine their location, and we caught our collective breath, the tall pine tree we were standing under burst into flames.

So much for our short rest.

Off we ran farther up the fire line behind the subdivision, toward the sound of chainsaws within the black, previously burned area.

The hotshot crews used their chainsaws to cut out a helispot, a small, temporary clearing, so a helicopter could land to drop or pick up firefighting personnel. The hotshots were cutting one in anticipation of needing to medevac the burned firefighter. The dozer, which had been working in the area, came back down the mountain to help clear a safety zone for the 120 or so firefighters who were all working in the vicinity of the subdivision. This new safety zone was within the area the Dude Fire already burned, so we would be in good shape. A helicopter was able to find its way through the smoke and extreme winds and picked up our patient. Now we found ourselves sitting in the safety zone, a smoke-filled clearing with nothing but ash and blackened trees, listening as the Bonita Creek subdivision burned.

I wanted to first check on my engine strike team personnel. I found them sitting together. They were all huddled up, talking about what had just happened. Once I knew they were good, I started walking around talking to the hotshot leaders to check in with them. In the fire organization, they didn't work for me, but I was the only middle-management position sitting in that safety zone. By luck, our division supervisors and operations chief were out of the area when things went to shit that day. I was the closest thing to a manager sitting in that safety zone.

The Phoenix news crews with their cameras began trying to interview the firefighters, filming all those folks sitting there in a daze, a fog of ash and smoke. We were all in shock. We knew the homes in the subdivision were burning. We could hear tires on some of the trucks exploding as they caught fire. Propane tanks were screaming like jet engines as they vented from the pressure of being in a fire. The explosions and sounds of destruction filled the air. The subdivision that had been my responsibility to protect would be gone.

It felt like a tremendous failure.

And I had no new information about the inmate crew. Ten shelters were deployed. We had rescued one, but there was no word on the remaining nineteen.

I had seen people perish before. I saw the terrible effects from unexpected accidents, affecting not only those directly involved but also those around the death or injury, who love and care for the person. As a first responder and a witness to the violence of death, I had been profoundly affected. It made me think of my own mortality and of a life I had not yet lived.

After an hour or so, the fire had cooled enough to venture back and assess the damage to our fire engines, vehicles, and equipment. We looked like ghosts coming out of the smoke back into the subdivision. Blackened faces, exhausted, dirty clothes, wandering back to a deserted subdivision where most of the homes were still burning. All the engines sustained some damage, but none were destroyed. I was amazed. Homes around the engines were gone, but the fire engines were mostly intact.

I had been driving my fire chief's command vehicle, and some of the lights were melted and the paint blistered. All I could think was that I would be in big trouble when I got back to my fire station. Funny what you think about during times like this.

Because the hotshot crews had left their vehicles a few miles away, we broke all the safety rules and had the hotshots load up on top of the fire engines. It was a sight to see each engine driving through the smoke with twenty firefighters sitting on top and hanging on to the tailboard. It reminded me of films of soldiers riding through the smoke on tanks during World War II. It was a scene I'll never forget.

In the meantime, Paul Gleason, the Zigzag hotshot leader, asked if we could go check on the Perryville inmate crew. I knew it had to be done, but I really didn't want to be the one to go see. I hadn't heard anything after the last radio broadcast about the ten shelters being deployed. I was in a weird state of mind. Exhausted from the lack of sleep, rummy in the head from breathing so much smoke for the last twenty hours or so, disoriented from having lost an entire subdivision, and still a bit freaked out since I hadn't heard from Rick on the water tender. I assumed he had made it, but I hadn't heard yet.

And now we were the closest firefighters to the firefighters in their shelters. It was an ominous feeling.

Paul and I walked down the fire line from the subdivision, past where we picked up the burned firefighter. After a short while we could see the aluminum shelters in disarray up ahead. I couldn't go any farther. Paul went down the rest of the way and spent some time looking around. I couldn't see and didn't want to see anything else, and started hiking back up to the subdivision.

When Paul arrived back at my truck in the subdivision, he was a changed man.

The sights he saw were things no one should witness. The human body is not meant to be seen after being burned in a fire. There were six dead firefighters. He was in shock. We were numb.

As we drove back to fire camp, we talked about what could have been done differently to protect those firefighters. In the following years, based on what he witnessed at the Dude Fire, Paul would develop a new set of firefighting guidelines that went on to be adopted by the national wildfire community. Those new standards demonstrated his extraordinary intelligence and insights and would lead to lives saved on future wildfires.

I, on the other hand, would deal with misplaced anger and decided that I would never again not speak up when I saw something not right on the fireground. It was a pivotal event in my life.

That night I went to sleep after working for about forty hours straight. I rolled out my sleeping bag on a piece of black plastic next to my truck and fell asleep, dead to the world.

Earlier that day I had been with six firefighters who were now dead. I had narrowly avoided being one of a few more dead firefighters myself. Immediately following a dramatic near-miss accident, you question everything. You're confused and can't quite think straight. I was unable to focus that night.

But that night my life changed for another reason. In my thirty-five years, it was the first night that I was able to fall asleep without anxiety and worry about how I would survive another day. I was so exhausted I couldn't think of one more worry in my life, the worry that had plagued me since childhood.

You see, although I was biologically a male, from my earliest memories, I knew I was really female. Every night of my life before bed I had prayed for guidance, strength, and wisdom, to survive another day as a man, knowing that in my heart I was truly a woman. It took the events of June 26, 1990, where six lives ended too soon—six lives not fully lived—to deplete my energy to the point that I couldn't even think of my core identity.

I slept.

2

HIDING IN PLAIN SIGHT

A COUPLE WEEKS LATER, THE Dude Fire was over—as far as the public was concerned. The family tragedies and funerals, the forever mourning and memories, the investigations and lawsuits, and the post-traumatic stress lingered.

We made the two-hour drive back to Prescott Valley. When we arrived at our fire department headquarters, we proceeded as normal: the crews washed and cleaned the fire trucks, restocked the gear and equipment—and the storytelling began. The Dude Fire had been local, state, and national news and on everyone's mind.

I was still in a disoriented mood, like when you're rubbing your eyes, trying to wake up after a long sleep. Kind of like when you're just a little bit hung over, going about your day with cobwebs in your head. I had been functioning just fine at the fire before returning home, running on adrenaline and going through the motions of a live firefight. I didn't have time to think too much about what had happened on June 26.

The rest of my time on the fire was hectic. We protected another subdivision along with some historical structures. We lost some buildings and we saved some, but the actions and activities surrounding those actions were familiar territory for me. Instinctual. Instinct allows you to ignore the weight on your back and keep moving. Firefighting made me feel normal. The familiar feeling of actively fighting the fire and protecting homes was like a warm blanket wrapped around my shoulders on a cool night. But the familiar comfort and escape of that warm blanket couldn't last forever. Soon I would have to think about and face what had happened—and what might happen.

That drive back to my fire department was when I began to think. The quiet of a long drive through the beautiful mountains of the northern Arizona landscape always put me in a prayerful mood. And I had a lot to pray about. My mind couldn't shake the thoughts of those six lives who would never again have a tender conversation with their kids, wives, or siblings. I had been one step away from being in that group. What conversations would I have missed with my loved ones? What dear life events would I have missed watching as my children grew up? I thought about and prayed for the six firefighters who were lost.

I thought about their families. I thought about the rescued firefighter still in the hospital burn unit and his family. I thought about my own actions. Could I have done more to save those lives? The easy answer was absolutely yes; I could have and should have done more. Survivor's guilt is real, and I continued to deal with that guilt for many years. My feelings were jumbled up, unclear. They would continue to unfold before me, but in the meantime, I had to face my fire chief.

A few years before, my chief tried to fire me while I was still a probationary firefighter. I never knew exactly why, but I assumed it was because I was never what he considered an "ideal candidate." I didn't look like the other guys. I was short and small, with manicured eyebrows and a wedge haircut that, while still regulation, betrayed my feminine side. And honestly, I probably didn't act like the other guys either. I was a good firefighter and hardworking, but I had a chip on my shoulder. I was always trying to prove I was as good as or better than the other firefighters.

When you've been carrying around the weight of "pretending" to be a man in this macho environment, it can mess you up. I had been overcompensating for years. Although I was trying to act tough and macho myself, those around me could see clearly that I was a bit too feminine and not masculine enough. It made for a dizzying, exhausting existence. Looking back, I'm amazed I was as successful as I was. It was hard to fit in and be "one of the guys" when I didn't feel like a guy. And I believe it was hard for the rest of the firefighters to embrace me as well.

So, I assumed my chief was going to be mad at me for some reason. I mean, the paint on his truck was blistered from the fire. The plastic taillights and the overhead red lights were melted. The truck was a mess—and this was his truck. As an ex-navy chief, he was a gruff and crusty type of guy. He always made sure we knew how important it was to care for the equipment.

Years before, when I was a probationary firefighter, my fire engine had pulled into the fire station next to the fuel pumps. "Fill it up," said my captain as he walked into the station.

I was very new on the job, anxious to make sure I was doing a good job and trying to prove myself worthy. It was hot, and riding around in the warm fire engine had nearly put me to sleep. When the captain barked out for me to fill the fuel tank, I got up from my seat and walked over to the fuel pumps. I made sure to use the diesel and began fueling up the engine. As I watched the little numbers turn on the fuel pump indicating one gallon, two gallons, three gallons, I followed the hose from the engine back to the pump. I was pumping diesel. Of course, I'm pumping diesel. This is a fire truck. I stopped the pump. Fifteen gallons pumped.

"Oh my gosh!" I froze.

I thought: *Three fire engines in the fleet have gas motors. They were the oldest fire engines. Was this one of them?* In my heat-induced drowsiness I couldn't think straight. And as a probationary firefighter, the chief didn't need much of an excuse to fire me. Had I just added fifteen gallons of diesel to the fuel tank instead of gasoline?

On duty inside the fire station was one of my best friends at the fire department, Rick (a different Rick than the one at Dude Fire). He and I were both probationary firefighters. We came on at the same time and were part of the same rookie class. I nervously walked into the station to find my friend.

"Hey, Rick, hmm . . . Engine 52, it's diesel, right? It's diesel, isn't it? It's not one of the old gas motors, right?" I was nervous because I already knew the answer.

Rick stared me. "No, 52 has a gas motor. It's one of the old ones. Did you put diesel in it?" he asked.

"Oh no, I'm in deep trouble," I said. "Chief is going to kill me."

I had to go find my captain and the chief. I was embarrassed and knew this was bad. Around the fire department, most of the firefighters were mechanically inclined. There was a hierarchy. If you were a gearhead, you had status. If you were a hunter, you had status. If you were a gearhead and a hunter, you were in the inner sanctum. I was neither a gearhead nor a hunter. And to prove my mechanical expertise, I had just added diesel to a gas engine's fuel tank.

I found the officers in the kitchen having a cup of coffee.

"Finish fueling the engine?" the captain asked.

I looked at my boots and then at the ceiling. "Uh, I think I put diesel in Engine 52's tank," I managed.

"You think? You think?!" the chief said, looking at me like I was an idiot. At that moment I felt like one.

"Yes, Chief, I mistakenly used diesel in Engine 52."

"Did you start the motor?"

"No, Chief, I realized my mistake and stopped pumping the fuel."

He looked at me with disgust. I was waiting to be yelled at, but he didn't yell. It was the way he was looking at me that made me want to go hide.

He just said, "Go drain the tank and try again with gasoline this time."

I felt like an idiot. It only reinforced the insecurity I tried desperately to hide. I should have known which motors were gas and which were diesel. Even though anyone could have made the same mistake, I felt so inadequate. I would have preferred if he had just yelled at me.

Rick helped me drain the tank. I had committed my first blunder while being a probationary firefighter. I knew I had to be more careful. That, or take up hunting.

If the chief thought we were mistreating the tools, equipment, or apparatus, he would come down on us hard. A scratch on any one of the fire engines was met with his wrath. We knew we were in trouble when a new scratch showed up on a rescue truck or fire engine. And now his truck, the truck I had been driving for two weeks, was seriously damaged. Blistered paint. Melted plastic on the red lights and trim. To add to my concerns, I had been sent to protect a subdivision, and most of it had burned down. And hanging heavy on my conscience were six dead firefighters.

Station 53 was located next to a city park in Prescott Valley. It was an open area with pretty views of Glassford Hill and the Bradshaw Mountains. Chief was waiting for me when I pulled into the rear parking lot at Station 53. I was caked in dirt, exhaustion weighing on my bones. I still smelled of smoke from the Dude Fire ten days prior. I braced myself, expecting to hear familiar derisive comments directed at me. He didn't exactly like me. I think he respected me, but he didn't exactly like me.

A few years before, my probation period as a new firefighter ended with a string of positive performance evaluations by the captains that I had rotated through. Each positive evaluation meant by the end of the year I would be made a permanent firefighter. But the chief had other plans. I was told by another firefighter that the chief was going to "extend" my probation. That could only mean one thing. If the fire department extended my probation, they could fabricate some evidence that I failed my probation and would fire me.

My stubbornness and familiarity with fighting for myself had prepared me for battle. I wouldn't be coming back on shift until several days after my probation ended. I would be ready. I wrote a letter to the chief stating that I had spoken to an attorney and that if they attempted to extend my probation, I would take them to court. Of course, I had not spoken to an attorney, but I would if it became necessary. In the letter I reminded him that all my quarterly performance evaluations had been above average. Furthermore, I was now officially off probation since my probation had ended several days before we were to meet. I was prepared.

When I went back to work, my captain called me into his office. The chief came in and handed me a letter stating that my probation would be extended by six months. I calmly read the letter. When I was finished, I pulled the letter I had written and gave it to him.

I watched him as he read my letter.

I watched as his face turned a bright, beet red. He stormed out of the office and into his fire chief command vehicle and tore out of the parking lot.

My captain just looked at me and said, "You should probably go find something to do around here and stay out of sight for a while."

My heart was racing. I didn't know for sure, but by the chief's reaction, I thought maybe I had won. I also knew the chief was pretty mad at me. I grabbed some yard tools and went outside to pull weeds around the fire station.

Within an hour or so, I saw the chief drive back to the station. I kept my head down and continued pulling weeds and raking.

"Hey Scopa, come here."

The chief was standing next to his vehicle, so I walked over to him holding my rake.

"I just came back from the attorney's office. You're off probation. He said I can't fire you now unless you kill someone."

I wanted to respond by saying, "Good to know my limits." Instead, I said, "OK, thanks," and I went back to my weed pulling. I was off probation.

That episode made me a firehouse lawyer. I studied the policies and procedures manual and eventually got on the union committee that was responsible for working with the chief and writing policies.

A few years later, the department was going to test for captain. That meant those firefighters who met all the criteria could go through the testing process for captain. We were opening a new fire station, and there would be three captains added to the roster along with twelve full-time firefighters. Normally I would have never considered testing for captain. I still felt too inexperienced to be promoted, but I knew the procedures manual. I knew the rules, and technically I was eligible to test.

I went to the headquarters station to talk to the chief. He was sitting in his office.

"Chief, I wanted to let you know that I plan on testing for captain next week," I said.

"What? You can't test. You don't have enough time on." He was indignant.

I spoke respectfully, but I stood my ground. I stated the exact policy on eligibility that proved my point. I was indeed eligible, and he knew it.

In reality, I was not ready to be a captain. Not quite. But I wanted to test. I wanted to prove to him and others on the department that I was good enough. So, I said, "I'll tell you what. You have my word that if I score in the top three, I promise not to take one of the captain positions. But I want to be on the list for a future captain's vacancy."

He looked at me hard.

"I give you my word, Chief," I said. "I will not take one of the positions if I score in the top three."

He was suspicious but finally grunted his agreement. I could tell he wasn't happy with me once again.

A year later, I was promoted to captain.

From those early days on the department, I was used to be being on guard around him, always ready to defend myself. But on this July day following the Dude Fire, standing behind Station 53, I was out of emotional reserves. I had nothing left to fight with.

As I pulled into the parking lot and exited the truck, he was there waiting.

"Hey Chief, the truck is kind of messed up," I said.

"Yeah, don't worry about it."

I looked up at him. Don't worry about it? The truck he entrusted to me comes back with blistered paint and melted lights, and he says don't worry about it? I just said "OK" and nothing else. I leaned against the truck while he stood next to me.

I don't remember exactly what was said next, but I began to tear up. I was crying because Chief seemed to be showing me some kindness. I was crying because for ten years on the fire department I had been holding so much emotion in. I was crying because I could only pretend to be macho for so long.

My tears leaked out around the corners of my eyes, my breath still steady. I had always tried to hide my emotions around my coworkers and the other officers at the department. I was usually successful—but not always. When Chief promoted me to captain a couple years before, I had teared up in his office. He had seen this vulnerability before. But as I was quietly crying next to him out there behind Station 53, he said to me, "You know, you're a hero."

All I could do was look at him, then down at my feet.

"I don't feel like a hero, Chief. Six firefighters are dead. I helped save one. This doesn't feel like being a hero to me. I only did what anyone else would do in the same situation."

What I didn't know was that news of the rescue had already hit the local and state newspapers. I would spend the next six months receiving awards from everyone from the governor to the Knights of Columbus.

The Dude Fire was the first wildfire in Arizona history with such a large loss of life and number of homes burned. It was big news, especially in our small community. And I was in the middle of it. In some ways, the public image of the hero fire captain would help camouflage my true self. I thought it gave me more cover. I mean, a hero firefighter can't possibly be transgender, right? Besides, back in 1990 most people had never heard that word, let alone knew what it meant. The Dude Fire might have bought me a couple more years before I couldn't hide anymore.

Over the years I tried to participate in activities and fit into roles that I thought would cover up my self-perceived lack of masculinity. I thought if I could play football in high school then I must not really be a woman inside—or at least no one would be able to see the real me. Of course, I was a poor football player, and I only played for two years. That attempt wasn't so successful.

On the other hand, when I first started fighting wildfires for the US Forest Service in 1974, that provided cover for me from a distance. Friends and family who knew I was fighting fires figured that maybe I was tough or masculine enough. Maybe I wasn't feminine after all. Although it wasn't talked about much while I was growing up, my mom had made a few comments through the years that proved to me she knew what I was struggling with.

But I know some of my coworkers on that first firefighting crew could see through my disguise. During my first summer fighting fires I was assigned to a hotshot crew, just like the hotshot crews years later that I would be working alongside on the Dude Fire. But in 1974 I showed up ill-prepared for the work and the ultramacho environment, not knowing what to expect.

The hotshot crew had all the macho bullshit of a high school football team on steroids. The locker room talk was what you might expect, but for me, I couldn't escape it. I couldn't just go home after eight hours and decompress. We worked sixteen-hour-plus days together on fires and then traveled shoulder-to-shoulder in an old truck for hours at a time. Whether riding in the truck or while working on the fire line, I found myself next to the same older firefighter day after long day. This guy particularly didn't like me.

Or maybe he liked me too much, I'm not sure which.

It was a common theme in my early life as a male. I think some people can see right through your pretense. And this one guy was relentless. When he knew no one could hear, he would tell me what a great figure I had.

It was never a compliment.

Among other things, I learned that I "had a fine ass," that he knew what he could do with my "fine ass," and "wouldn't you enjoy yourself too?" When you think you're hiding your true self successfully by being a tough firefighter and a fellow firefighter is talking about your figure and taking you in a sexual manner, it makes it hard to keep up the pretense. When things like this happened to me, which they did from time to time, it was as if someone could see through my facade. It scared me and caused me to wonder if they could see through my cover, who else could? The worst part about it was, it felt like the people who might have gotten a glimpse of the real me were the very ones I would least want to know.

I often felt like my cover was blown. If I had been a character in a TV show spy thriller, someone should have been yelling, "Abort, abort!" But I persisted. I kept up the charade because really, what choice did I have?

3

THE SCIENCE EXPERIMENT

WHAT CHOICE *DID* I HAVE? I grew up as the youngest of four children with Italian immigrant parents. From the outside, our home life seemed fairly ordinary, but for a young child, the confusion of gender identity is disorienting. You don't know what to do, who to talk to, or even what to say if you did have someone to talk to.

In the decades since, I've heard people express their concern, especially for children, about the seemingly "new" attention on transgender people. People assume that a young child can't conceivably know their gender identity at a young age. They assume that a child doesn't—or can't possibly—know their core identity until their late teens. I've been told this by my own family members. Well-meaning friends express concern that parents of transgender children are allowing their child to transition at a young age.

"How could a child possibly know they're transgender?" they ask me.

When I hear those comments or questions my mind drifts back to my childhood self. I don't recall how old I was exactly, but I remember when I moved from my crib to the big bed. It was during this time period that I had a conscious fear that something was wrong with me.

Everyone was treating me like a boy, but I knew the difference between boys and girls—and I was supposed to be a girl. It causes a child great anxiety and fear when they're four, five, or six years old. At that age you're beginning to understand not only the world but also yourself. That anxiety only gets worse as you grow up and grow into a body in which you don't belong, and it has the potential to cause great harm to yourself and those around you.

So, what choice did I have? When you're a child, you do what your parents say to do. Or at least, in my old-fashioned immigrant parents' home we did what Mom and Dad told us. I can clearly remember asking my older sister to paint my nails as a child. I loved how my fingers looked all pretty when freshly painted. I have a vivid memory of being told that I would no longer be allowed to wear nail polish. There was no discussion. There was no explanation other than "boys don't have painted nails."

I can remember my dad ignoring the conversation. My sister walked away, and my mom told me in no uncertain terms that I couldn't go to school with nail polish on. I don't recall ever arguing about it. I couldn't argue about it. I was raised to do what I was told. I was an obedient child. It was the beginning of my acquiescing to those who were in authority over me, to my future wife, and to society in general.

I was born in 1955. Trying to buck the system in 1960 or when I started high school in 1969 just wasn't going to happen. If I had been born thirty years later, my whole life might have been different, but this was my reality. Maybe I did have choices, but I didn't see them then, and even today, looking back, I still don't see them. People certainly transitioned throughout the 1970s and were able to live as their true selves, but within my environment, with the emotional tools in my possession, transitioning wasn't possible for me. I thought the cost of those choices were too great. I didn't realize the cost went up every year and eventually it would almost cost me my life.

According to Lexico, the term *gender dysphoria* is "the condition of feeling one's emotional and psychological identity to be at variance with one's birth sex," and it was unknown back in the 1960s and early '70s. Even language that predates that current term was completely unknown to me at the time.

How can anyone know what personal choices exist without even having a vocabulary to describe what's going on within themselves?

I began conducting my own research during my bachelor's program in 1973. Being on campus at Arizona State gave me access to the cavernous library, and I spent as much time studying up on my personal condition as I did on my schoolwork. What I found disturbed me: gender identity disorder, what is now often known as gender dysphoria, was considered a psychiatric disorder. According to these books, I was either a sexual deviant or I was mentally ill. There were some scholarly articles and books that strayed from those two themes but for the most part, the world viewed me as either sick or a pervert.

What choice did I have?

I learned to adapt to this "boy's life" when I was a child. Being told I couldn't have my nails painted was the beginning of a conscious, outward shift. At some point in grammar school, I read a *Reader's Digest* article about Christine Jorgenson, the famous transgender actress who transitioned back in the 1950s. She was the first person to become widely known for having sex reassignment surgery, and the public nature of her transition broke ground for the rest of us who came afterward. Once I heard about her, I felt I finally had a choice. I knew that transitioning to be a woman was an option, an alternative that I didn't even know I had before—a distant possibility but a possibility nonetheless. During my nightly prayers before bed, I promised myself, "Well that's it, I'll transition when I get older, and I can finally be a girl." But what seemed possible to a twelve-year-old child seemed impossible as I got older.

I have a vivid memory of playing by myself in the front yard of our family home. Sometimes I sat, shielded under our citrus trees, my mind wandering. I questioned why I felt the way I did. I wondered if my mom understood.

"She never says much to me about it," I thought. "But does she know?"

Sitting there in the shade of a big old grapefruit tree, I began to convince myself that I was part of some science experiment. Is there something going on that no one is telling me? I kept thinking that at some point, Mom and Dad were going to call me into the living room and tell me the truth. I had been a part of a giant science experiment, they would say, and now I was going to get a special pill, and I would be fixed. I didn't even care how I would be fixed. I just wanted to be normal. Boy or girl, I didn't even care which. Just make me feel normal. Years later, I still wondered if there was something they knew but never told me.

As a teenager, it became clear that gender roles were absolute in our household, but my mom allowed me to stretch the roles to some degree. Using different excuses and without any admonishment from my mom, I began embroidery. I loved the colors of the floral designs that I sewed. I loved the finished look, and my sister and I were able to enjoy it together.

My mom was just happy that I wasn't causing trouble like my older brothers. She even taught me how to sew, and I started sewing tops for myself. I found patterns that were "unisex," and I made and wore some very feminine blouses. Back in the early '70s, I could pass off as being a hippie. Through bell-bottom jeans, floral embroidered tops, and my longish hair, I began to feel better about myself. Not great, because I still had to pretend to be a boy, but more myself.

The worst thing about my high school years was the feeling of exclusion. The girls hung out together, and the boys hung out together. Some of my best friends were girls, yet there were times when I couldn't be a part of the group.

I longed to be a part of that group. I wanted to have my hair brushed and braided like the rest of the girls. It physically hurt not to have the intimacy of close female friendships. A true heartache. The pain in my chest was no less painful, no less real. I didn't want to be thought of as a boy. Yet I had to be a boy. I couldn't see any alternative. I would try to thread the needle: find a sweet spot between being a regular ordinary male and transitioning to being a female. I started trying to thread that needle as a teenager and continued for another twenty-five years.

Teenage hormones and relationships made life even more difficult to navigate. Throughout high school and college I dated girls because even if I was mixed up and sewing my blouses, I thought I was mostly successful at being a boy. I knew I wasn't gay, but inside I longed to be a normal teenage girl in a typical relationship with a boy. Sound confusing? Imagine what it felt like to my fifteen-year-old self. I remember seeing my friends holding hands together walking across the quad at school.

Another heartache. One more "normal" experience that I couldn't have. One more need that I'd never be able to quench.

I didn't think I had a choice, and in hindsight, I still don't see one. Had I tried to do something different, to live as my true self, I would have been sent to an institution or sent to the priest to have the devil cast from me.

But in the meantime, my Christian faith helped me. I had someone to pray to, and I felt the very real presence of God in my life. I knew God listened to me, and I endeavored to be a good person, to follow scripture and all that entailed. Of course, I failed every day like all well-intentioned Christians, but it was my foundation, my inspiration. I never saw any discrepancies between my religious beliefs and the reality of me being transgender. I knew God had made me this way. I assumed my challenge was to figure out how to live a true Christian life while being the me God created. Scripture gave me the values that would guide me for the rest of my life.

So how does a sixteen-year-old "boy" struggling with gender identity deal with life? In 1971 I found a middle ground through the numbers of female friends that fulfilled some of my social needs. But by then, just four years later, I had given up on my twelve-year-old's dream of transitioning. At sixteen I was sure that it was not possible, and that it would never be possible. My parents would kill me before letting me transition—and I use that description with only a little exaggeration. I have no doubt that had I told them who I was and how I felt, I would have been beaten.

There were no examples to follow. No role models other than Christine Jorgenson in *Reader's Digest*. I figured I was going to have to toughen up, pull myself together, and be a man. It's hard not to laugh at that idea now. It was hopeless, but I saw few options for my continued survival.

My parents were simple, bighearted people. They enjoyed having lots of people over to our home for big noisy meals with wonderful Italian food. My parents trusted everyone to be equally kind and good. We had a family acquaintance that was a single man who did some business with my parents. He routinely invited me to go spend the weekend with him at his little getaway in Mexico.

"Why don't you go with Mr. Smithers* to Mexico?" my mom would ask.

I might have been thirteen or fourteen years old at the time. My parents were so trusting. But my young mind knew that something was weird about Mr. Smithers. I was never sure about it, but I knew I didn't want to go with him for the weekend. Today, no parent would allow their young child to go away on their own to a foreign country with only an unmarried male chaperone. But this was 1970, and my parents weren't worldly or suspicious. Yet that request put me on edge; it made me aware that I had to be on guard for my own safety. Over the years, many similar experiences reinforced that belief.

All teenagers have a difficult time even in the best of circumstances. It's a time of growth, change, and differentiation from parents. Kids make mistakes and get into trouble. High school can be a positive time and place as well, and as messed up as my life might have been, I had a lot of fun during my high school years. I began my own somewhat traditional rebellion from my parents, staying out late, experimenting with drinking, adventuring with friends, and getting into the typical hijinks that teens get into.

I attended a relatively small Catholic high school in Phoenix. Our teachers were a combination of nuns, priests, and lay teachers. It was one of the most positive and affirming environments I have been in. Internally I struggled with my gender daily, wishing for, praying for some divine intervention to magically transform my exterior into the girl I knew I was inside. But aside from that one "minor" detail, I had a good gig going on.

One of the activities I found satisfaction in was the Phoenix Mayor's Youth Advisory Board. Back in the early '70s, each high school was able to appoint two representatives to be on the board. I don't even know how I came to represent our school, but it was an important development for me. We took on projects that had some social significance. Drug abuse was one of the issues, and we raised money to help stem the rising tide of drug use by hosting activities that were thought to distract teens from the appeal of drugs. (Did it work? Was the reasoning valid? Hard to say—but this was 1972.) One way we raised money was to bring in big-name musical acts, and through sponsorships with

---

* Pseudonym

large local businesses, the Mayor's Youth Advisory Board began putting on concerts. We were able to bring in Seals and Crofts, the Beach Boys, and others. It was a pretty cool thing for any junior in high school—let alone one hiding their gender. It was an amazing, successful distraction.

Being involved with city politics and the mayor's office in a very cursory way, I was exposed to other political efforts and a different social circle. Sometime in my junior year, I was asked to be on the Phoenix Mountains Preservation Commission.

Back in the early 1970s the mountains within the municipality of Phoenix had no protections. With few zoning requirements in place, private landowners could build into and develop the mountainside. It was a concern to many residents that the beauty of and access to the mountains would be lost if not protected. So a city commission was established, and I served on that city commission for a couple years. There were lawsuits, zoning changes, and other efforts made, but the only real way to save the mountains was to purchase key parcels of land and keep the houses from moving up the mountain. "Save the Mountains" was a local rallying cry in 1972. We made and sold bumper stickers, held rallies, and brought in big-name entertainers and whatever else we could think of to preserve the mountains. Now in 2021, retired and spending my winters as a snowbird in Phoenix, I still enjoy and appreciate the work we did almost fifty years ago.

As a retiree, I enjoy riding my bike around town through bike paths and trails along the canal system. Back in the 1970s there were no bike or pedestrian trails along the waterways. That was another effort I worked on with the Parks Department. Phoenix is crisscrossed with irrigation canals operated by the Salt River Project. When I was a youngster grow-ing up in Phoenix, the dirt banks along the side of the canals were our bicycle routes through town. Kids could stay off the streets and go from one neighborhood to another on the trails. But legally, those trails were off-limits to bike riders or joggers. There were no-trespassing signs and cables to stop access. The teens from the Mayor's Youth Advisory Board worked with the Parks Department to open those routes for everyone's use. The battle wasn't won while I was still on the board, but fifty years later those paved bike paths are part of what makes life good for me now. Hiking in the preserve and using the bike routes are like revisiting my old teenage efforts.

I wasn't a great student, but I had a good attitude and a desire to be involved in important things. When I look back at the privilege and freedom I had, I'm amazed. If I had a meeting downtown at City Hall during my third-period English class with Sister Mary, I went to the school office to tell Mrs. Larkin that I would be back before lunch. I wheeled out of the school parking lot in my little purplish-blue dune buggy with a white interior and headed to my meeting. I had no idea how unique my situation was. If not for the tight-knit community environment I was living in, I don't think I would have flourished like I did. Years later, my mom told me that she went to talk to the school principal to see if it was acceptable for me to miss so many classes. Apparently, the principal assured my mom I was getting a good education down at City Hall.

As much as I enjoyed all these activities I still had to pretend. I had to put the face of a certain kind of boy forward. I knew how to dress and how to act depending upon the surroundings. I realized that to be successful, whatever that meant in a given situation, all I had to do was act, talk, and dress a certain way. I became a chameleon.

One day I was asked to speak to a parents' group at one of the local schools. I don't recall what they were meeting about or why I was supposed to talk to them, but at the time, that's the sort of thing I found myself doing. I remember speaking off the cuff for about half an hour. After the meeting, some of the parents came up to me, gushing about how they wished I were dating their daughter. I was an excellent chameleon. I sincerely loved the work I did back then, and I was committed to the causes. But I was still acting.

As easy as it was to play a role on the outside, the emotional exhaustion and inner battle was hard to tune out. I turned to alcohol, drinking in excess trying to escape from my own pain. It is not an exaggeration to say it was probably a miracle I didn't die or end up in the hospital from excessive drinking. I was running from myself, trying to ignore the confusion of being a girl inside my teenage boy body. There is no way to describe it other than to say it was disorienting. Imagine the confusion, the fear, the desperation of anyone in that situation. Anyone in that situation feels totally alone. No one to talk to. Not even the language to describe what's going on. I never even saw anyone that was like me.

One evening I finally did see another transgender person other than Christine Jorgenson. I was in college, and, having finished my homework, I came out of my bedroom and sat down on the couch to watch TV with my mom. She had turned on *The Merv Griffin* show. On this night, a young lady in her mid-thirties came on the screen. Canary Conn was very pretty with long blond hair—and she was a transgender woman. The entire program was all about trans people. She talked freely about her life: how she grew up as a confused boy, eventually transitioning to being female and having surgery to complete her change. I sat there with my mom listening to the only trans person I had ever seen live on TV. This was incredibly significant for me. I had never seen a transgender woman before and here was one right on the TV screen. She talked about her life. She spoke about how young she was when she knew something was wrong. When the program was over, I started to say something to my mom. Before I could utter one syllable, she started to get up from the couch, looked away from me, and said, "Don't get any ideas."

For the first time in my life, someone verbally acknowledged that I was struggling with being a girl in a boy's body.

She knew.

It was scary that she knew. But she knew.

And still, I was going to have to deal with this on my own.

It felt like my choice had been made for me. I was going to have to try and be a relatively normal male. I would never be normal, but I had to pretend.

I had a facade to maintain. I had to try and find a way to survive. I didn't even know what that meant exactly, I just knew I wouldn't and couldn't be like other men. I had no role model, no example to follow. I assumed I was the only one trying to thread the needle between male and female. I would be riding on faith alone. I dealt daily with the duality of enjoying my life and hating my life. My future was uncertain. It was like looking down the highway and only seeing thick fog. But I had been driving fifty miles per hour down the highway for a few years and hadn't wrecked yet, so I would keep on driving.

4

KILLING BIRDS

BY THE TIME I WAS in college at Arizona State, I accepted that I would have to live out the rest of my life as a male. It would be tough, but, by God, I was tough. I spent my summers fighting fires and that was proof, right?

I mean, you can't be some sissy boy if you're fighting forest fires, I reasoned to myself at the time.

No way. I was strong and tough, and I would be a man.

I was fairly successful, but not completely. Sometimes someone recognized the real me, and that always freaked me out. There were moments when I thought I was doing my best imitation of a man, yet somehow someone still seemed to see through the disguise, and my confidence was momentarily broken. I was shaken, exposed. I recovered and put the mask back up and moved on. I sort of convinced myself—and most of those around me—that I was just a regular guy.

My love for the outdoors pushed me to study natural resource management. I felt a strong spiritual connection to being in the desert and in the mountains. Growing up I spent as much time as I could hiking, backpacking, hunting, and generally messing around in the great outdoors. It was and still is where I do my best praying. So, it only made sense that I would study how to care for God's creation. That's how I looked at it: I would get a job where I could have some influence in taking care of the environment. For a college student interested in working on the land, spending my summers as a US Forest Service wildland firefighter killed three birds with one stone.

First, I earned decent money due to all the overtime firefighting. In 1974 I was making $3.12 per hour. Not very much, but when you're working eighty hours a week and getting paid time and a half for forty of those hours, that's not bad—especially since in the early 1970s, tuition at Arizona State was about $150 per semester. I lived at home throughout college, so my expenses were minimal. Summertime firefighting was a good way to build up my savings account to last at least partway through the winter. During the school year I worked weekends at a plant nursery, something I'd done since I was fifteen and stuck with for years to come.

Spending summers working for the US Forest Service would look good on my resume, since the agency was a likely employer for me once I graduated from college. If I kept spending my summers working for them, I figured I'd be a shoo-in for a full-time job in a couple years. Of course, that was the plan, and plans don't always come through. But in the early '70s it seemed a reasonable strategy.

But perhaps more important, firefighting gave me "good cover." I needed to convince myself and others around me that I was a typical guy. If I was worried that people didn't think I acted like a normal guy, being a firefighter might make up for people's suspicions about my behavior and looks

But there was one other reason I was fighting wildfires, a reason more important than any of the others.

I loved it. It was exciting. It was cool. It was awesome.

It was also miserable work.

Wildland firefighting is hot and sweaty with little glamour. It's not like working for a city fire department, where you work hard for a short while and the public sees you and gives you instant kudos and admiration. Wildland firefighters do their work where few people can see. Hours and days of backbreaking work with little excitement. The work is often hidden on hillsides, away from subdivisions filled with homes and city fire trucks. What people see are the city fire engines protecting the homes. Cutting brush and trees with hand tools and scraping the earth to build fire lines doesn't conjure up the same public image of running into a burning building. It's not what most people would think of as heroic or dramatic, but it is, in fact, how homes and lives are saved.

But when it is exciting, it's wildly exciting. Sometimes way too exciting.

I'll always remember my first fire. My hotshot crew was building a fire line up a hill. There was a dry creek below us, and the fire was burning right there in the drainage next to our fire line. It was hot. We were flanking the fire as we built line up the canyon. I had no idea what was going on, and it was hard to pay attention to the actual work I was supposed to be doing as I felt the heat on my face and the adrenaline of the moment. All I could do was look at everything going on. I was in awe.

Every few minutes the crew boss would yell at us, "Slurry coming in! Everyone DOWN!"

That was the order to get down on our bellies.

Today we refer to the planes and jets delivering aerial retardant as air tankers, but back then they were B-17 Slurry Bombers, and when they came in to drop, they came in low—very low. Those old reciprocating aircraft engines rumbled so much, the ground shook when they went over. There we were, lying on the ground with our heads facing in the direction that the plane was coming from in case the slurry hit us. One hand on our helmets in case we got hit, one hand holding our hand tool—our axes, our Pulaskis, our shovels—out at arm's length so we wouldn't be injured if the slurry hit us. Slurry, which we now refer to as *retardant*, is heavy, with the consistency of pancake batter. If you were hit by a direct load of slurry at a low altitude, you'd be ripped apart. The old training films showed a fire engine on a runway purposely struck by a low, direct hit. The fire engine was rolled up into a little ball of metal after being hit by the heavy red liquid. Thankfully, retardant is dropped from much higher altitude now, between 170 and 200 feet. But in the 1970s, the height was half that.

As the ancient World War II plane rumbled overhead and the ground quaked, I wanted to watch, to yell at the top of my lungs "AWESOME!" But you weren't supposed to watch the plane because you were supposed to have your head down—just in case. Still, I always snuck a peek and risked being yelled at by the boss. It was the most exciting thing I had ever been a part of at age nineteen.

I was hooked.

A year or two later, on a brush fire that I was now in charge of, a slurry bomber circled our fire. In those days we didn't always have radio communications with the pilot in the plane. There were no other fire aircraft around to help relay communications between the bomber and those of us on the ground.

This was a routine problem, so some of the slurry bombers had a red flashing light and siren mounted on the belly of the aircraft, like the lights and sirens on a police car. The pilots would make a few dry practice runs to find the best line to make their drop. When they were finally ready to come in hot and drop their load, the pilot would turn on their red light and siren. When we saw the red light and heard the siren, we knew this was it. He was coming in hot. This was when we ran for cover and got on our bellies.

But this one time, something seemed different. I stood there on the ridgetop in the thick brush burning around us with my little Kodak Extralight camera, ready to snap a picture. The pilot was so low I could see him laughing through the cockpit window. He gave me a wigwag wave with his wings and flew on by. He was just having fun at our expense, watching us scramble. He was out of slurry. He wasn't making another drop. I stood there and watched him fly by, laughing at us.

What a job this was for me at twenty years old! I was outdoors, driving a fire engine, fighting fires, watching World War II aircraft make the ground under our feet rumble. Truthfully, I didn't even need the first three reasons to do this job, though they were great justification. I loved being a firefighter.

This was more than my summer job; it was my escape. I didn't have to think about deeper issues if I was preoccupied. If I was excited by my work and challenged both physically and mentally, I had no time to think about life's greater problems. Who had time to worry? I would worry and say my prayers when I went to sleep that night, exhausted from the action.

I like to describe to people that living as a transgender person is like being covered by a fabric over your entire body. That cloth had the male persona, the accepted and dictated male "look," creating the person people expected you to be. As long as the fabric was intact no one could see the real you underneath.

A real twenty-year-old girl lived just under the fabric, but no one could see her—not truly. Every once in a while, few could see under or through it. In my twenties, that cloth covering was in pretty good shape. There were no tears or rips in the cloth. I thought I was impervious. But if you wear the same fabric for days and years and decades, it's eventually going to wear out.

One of the other ways I provided for my undercover assignment was by dating girls. I dated a lot of girls in high school and through college. I had steady girlfriends. Some were serious and some were not, but it reinforced who I was: a naturally social person who loved being around women. Only two girls through high school and college gave me any indication that they doubted my masculinity. Otherwise, I felt fairly confident in my cover story.

During my junior year of college, I met the girl I would marry and have two children with. Regardless of my gender issues, I was in love with her. We had similar backgrounds. We were both Catholic and had attended similar Catholic schools all the way through high school. Her parents even had some social connections with mine. Life was confusing, but she helped me feel normal. At that point in our relationship, she didn't know the rest of the story, but she loved me too. She loved who she thought I was.

Since I had already made the decision that I would live my life as a male, all would be good. I was sure of it. It had to be. What other choice did I have?

I made the decision to continue down this road, traveling sixty miles per hour on this highway of my life. The fog was heavy, but this was the only way to continue. Yet car wrecks in the fog are pretty normal, and those car wrecks have devastating effects.

I decided that even though I loved firefighting I could not continue to work in such a hostile environment. I was bullied and always had to be on guard, worried about what some redneck would do or say to me. Even though I loved being out in the wildlands of Arizona and I loved firefighting fires, I needed a safer, more comfortable environment to work in. The following summer, I changed locations and went to work on a fire engine at another station. My experience on a hotshot crew brought me some status. My new boss assumed I must be a pretty good firefighter if I held my own on a hotshot crew. That was a completely false assumption on his part. The dynamics on the crew I had come from were such that I received no training, no coaching, and no mentoring. I was continuously told to "shut up and dig," to cut a fire line on a wildfire. There I was nothing more than a "Pulaski motor," a machine that cuts fire line, and a favorite put-down on the crew. I was expected to be quiet, not complain, not question anything, or dare pick up my head from the dirt I was digging in. The crew boss wouldn't even give me my own line pack—a military-style web belt with shoulder straps, allowing one to carry necessities such as food, canteens of water, spare socks, and other items. I actually had to go to a US Army surplus store to buy my own pack, belt, and shoulder harness.

I was just happy to move on, to be able to still fight fires and be out of the horrible environment I endured the previous summer. When I arrived at the new station the following summer, they had a line pack waiting for me.

In some ways, fighting wildfires in the 1970s was nothing like it is today. Currently, a firefighter must have specific formal training and experience to be considered qualified in certain positions. A wildland firefighter is required to carry a "red card" that documents their certifications. A promotion to fire captain or fire engine operator requires at least five years, if not more, to be qualified. But in 1975, I was a warm body who had just come from a hotshot crew. So surely I qualified to drive and operate the fire engine. And on the engine captain's day off, I would be operating on my own with no adult supervision. The idea of this makes me laugh now. It should make any experienced wildland firefighter cringe and duck, waiting for an accident to happen.

Fortunately, even though I had received no training the previous summer, I spent a lot of time observing and trying to ask questions.

Unfortunately, most often my questions were ignored, or I was told to shut up. Slowly, though, I had started to piece things together on my own.

Once while cutting fire line midslope (horizontally positioned part way up a mountain) on a mountain side with the fire just above us, trees and logs on fire kept rolling downhill over our fire lines. One piece of large burning material hit one of the firefighters and injured him. The burning materials started a fire below us. Now the fire that had been burning above us was also quickly coming up the hill at us from below, threatening the safety of the entire crew.

"RTO, RTO! Everyone back to the rockslide," yelled the crew boss.

He was telling us to reverse tool order. When creating a fire line you cut first and dig, then scrape at the end. Now those of us who had scraping tools and were clearing the fire line took up the lead, with the chainsaws and cutting tools following behind.

The twenty hotshots ran back down the fire line we had just made, back to a small rock escarpment with no fuel on it. It wouldn't be big enough to escape the flames that were now rushing up at us from the hillside below. We began cutting the brush and trees around the rocky area. I threw brush and tree branches over the side of the rock cliff while the flames licked at our little clearing. We barely escaped the flames as we sat in our hurriedly constructed safety zone while the fire burned around us. It was a very close call.

I didn't have to be a genius to figure out that cutting a midslope fire line was dangerous. I learned by watching the fire, the weather, the vegetation, and the topography, as well as by watching our tactics and seeing the results. It wasn't the most efficient way to learn, but by the next summer I could make some reasonable decisions on tactics and strategies while being in charge of a small crew on a fire. The fire chief in me now winces when I think about how I started out. But she's a little amazed too.

Despite all my observation, I still struggled to figure out why the guys didn't like me. It didn't piece together as easily. With every new fire station, every new opportunity, I found it just as difficult to become close with my fellow firefighters. Was it because of the way they perceived me, or was it because I carried this invisible weight like a chip on my shoulder and acted like a jerk? It was probably a bit of both. Why didn't the crew boss give me some government-issued gear to use at work? Why did he make me go buy my own? I experienced a similar antagonistic attitude by supervisors for much of my early career. Eventually, that attitude toward me would change. Not completely, but it would be much better.

In 1975 I found myself running a firefighting crew on several different fires. If our local wildfires grew larger than the fire engine could handle, the local Forest Service station would gather up all the other workers from around the ranger station and form them up into a fire hand crew. Many of the men working back then were schoolteachers off for the summer. Some of them were retirees just working in a seasonal position to make a few extra dollars. These guys normally worked on the recreation crew emptying garbage cans and cleaning out the toilets in the campgrounds. But when fires got big and all the regular district firefighters were already assigned, they became firefighters. Unlike a hotshot crew, this group wasn't elite. It wasn't well trained, and it had me as a crew boss. But I figured out what to do. And we managed to be successful. No one ever got hurt, and we put in miles of hand line. I was smart enough to take advice and counsel from some of the older men on the crew. They knew I had come from the hotshot crew the year before and was now working on the local fire engine, so they assumed I knew what I was doing. In a way, I did. That one miserable summer on a hotshot crew had set me up for some level of success.

After the summer was over and I returned to school to continue my studies, I walked with my head held high. Another successful summer to prove I was capable. I had money in the bank and more experience to help me land a job after graduation. I'd created more cover for my undercover life assignment.

Three dead birds with some real excitement and fun.

5

DRIVING BLIND

IN THE WINTER OF 1977 I was looking forward to graduating in a few months with my degree from Arizona State University. It felt like quite an accomplishment for a mediocre student like me. My family was also dealing with personal tragedy. My sister—my oldest and dearest sibling—was dying of cancer. She was only thirty-one years old. Growing up, she had been my ally, my protector against my two older brothers who were between us in age. She was nine years older than I was, and I had depended on her my entire life. She was one of a kind. Everyone who knew her loved her. She was a big part of all my friends' lives. When she got sick, my mom and I took turns driving her to and from her cancer treatments and caring for her infant daughter and toddler son while her husband went to work to pay the bills. It was a labor of love—and fear. To care for my cherished sister in her final days was an honor and an unbelievable shock to my inner core.

We lost Kay in June, just six months after she was diagnosed with cancer. Losing Kay was incredibly difficult for me. Even though we never talked about my gender issues, she knew. Besides painting my nails when I was little, we brushed each other's hair, compared her needlepoint with my embroidery, and always had a very close relationship. We were more like sisters. She knew that sometimes I experimented with her makeup and wigs, but it was seldom mentioned. She left a hole in our family dynamic that would have a lasting and negative impact on my life.

Her tragic death was made even more horrific because she left behind her husband, an infant daughter, and a toddler son. It would be the first of many tragic deaths that I would witness or endure in my life, and seeing people die became foundational to who I was and what I believed in. Seeing death made me value life even more. It made me want to tell people not to sweat the small stuff. I began to realize how important it was for me to be my real self, while fighting the urge to sacrifice that self for the comfort of my family. To this day I don't know what the right answer is.

Watching someone you love die is as hard as you can imagine it is. If you haven't witnessed it, you couldn't understand it. I was trying to graduate from college, carrying more than 20 semester hours of course work that last semester. Besides taking care of my dying sister and her children, carrying a huge course load at Arizona State, and working twenty hours a week, I was figuring out how to simply survive. It was a stressful semester.

And I was engaged to be married.

Getting engaged was just one more layer on that horrible year, adding to all the stress. I didn't know if I should be getting married at all. How was I going to do this? Could I bear all that marriage meant?

I was missing months of work as this stress compounded, manifesting itself in an illness. I had to be seen at the university health center for intestinal problems. The doctor simply said I was suffering from stress and to try and work less and relax. Just work less and relax. Right, sure, no problem. Thinking about it forty-five years later, I'm amazed that I survived it myself.

Earlier that year while driving from Flagstaff back to Phoenix after a weekend playing in the snow, my girlfriend told me that it was time to get married. At this point in my life, I had every intention of staying male until I was dead, one way or another. So when she said we should get married, I said OK. In order to maintain a more traditional facade, she gave me her grandmother's ring so at a later date I could formally ask her to marry me and give her the ring.

Through the fog on my proverbial highway, I could see danger up ahead. I was driving too fast, and the fog was too thick. I had to be going seventy miles per hour now, driving blind. I didn't know how to stop this trip I was on. She deserved to know what was in my heart—who I really was before we got married. It would be dishonest for me to hide this critical, vital information. I decided to bare my soul to this beautiful young woman who wanted to marry me.

One evening I did it. I finally came out and told her who I was.

I was more nervous than I had ever been in my life. I had never just come out and told anyone who I really was inside. I was twenty years old and had never openly talked about my life, my feelings, my needs and fears and desires and confusion. I didn't even have the right language to describe who I was. I was desperately afraid. I wasn't just scared that she would reject me. I accepted that rejection was a reasonable response to the news I would tell her. In fact, being rejected by her would have been the healthiest outcome that could have happened after I told her. I was scared because I had never purposely showed anyone what was hiding inside me. I had never lifted that fabric covering to show someone who was underneath. It made me dizzy to say the words. I tried to ease into the conversation because I was too scared to begin. But I did start, and as I set out to give more details of who I was and explain all my feelings, she quickly cut me off.

She didn't want to hear the specifics of who I was. As long as I didn't have any plans to make changes—to transition—she was OK.

I was shocked. I thought we'd have a long, tearful conversation where she'd ask me questions and I'd try to explain. And there were tears—on my part. She told me that the best way to deal with this issue was to not talk about it.

"The more we talk about it, the worse it will be," she said.

I felt like I was swerving through a pile of crashed cars on that fog-shrouded freeway, like a drunk driver narrowly missing the wreck in front of him. It was a familiar refrain, one I'd internalized since I understood the truth about who I was: don't talk about it and everything will be OK.

I had no idea how that was going to work out. How will it be OK by not talking about it? Admittedly, it wasn't much different than my own coping mechanism for the last twenty years. But now this head-in-the-sand approach included another person, and eventually my two dear, sweet children.

Years later in couples therapy, I would learn that I was always too quick to acquiesce in my relationships because I was afraid of conflict. I trusted her so much that I tended to put her on a pedestal. I had respected and trusted her intellect and power. And if she thought we could make it by not talking about the elephant in my closet, she must have been right. I had my doubts, but not completely showing someone, even her, what was under my fabric covering was easier than dealing with the most life-altering issue in my world. So, I went along. What choice did I have?

We were married in May, a month before my sister passed away. It was a traditional wedding. I had little to do with the planning. I was still trying to graduate while babysitting my niece and nephew and taking turns driving my sister to her medical treatments. The fog on my highway had permeated every bit of my waking life. How was I going to deal with being married to a woman and all those expectations? The person in my family whom I was closest to was dying. I still had to pass my courses to get my degree. I had to find a job. I had to perform a life.

Kay's death later that summer shook everyone in my family, and I now had to figure out how to navigate through life without my champion. Even though I had never spoken the words out loud about my gender identity, I knew Kay knew who I really was. I kept waiting for the right moment to talk to her about it. Despite everything else, I felt the opportunity growing closer and closer—until it never came. It was like the book had closed, and I could never open it again.

When you're in the fog, you don't really know it—you're not aware of how thick it really is. You aren't a good judge of what you can't see. Now, more than forty years later, I realize I was like a drunk stumbling around. The only difference between a drunk in the gutter and me was that I would do what I was told. And I kept doing what I was told: what my family thought I should do, what my wife told me to do, what society expected me to do. I was getting pretty good at driving too fast through the fog.

After the wedding, my sister's death, and my graduation, I had to find a full-time job. After four summers of working for the US Forest Service, I thought there must be an easier place to work. The last few summers were much better than the summer on the hotshot crew, but it was still an unhealthy environment for me. I was still treated poorly by management. I never knew for sure why that was, but looking back, I chalk it up to their discomfort around me, which boiled down to prejudice and my resentment of repeatedly being treated differently. The agency offered me a permanent job in a remote location, but I had flashbacks of my summer on the hotshot crew. I feared being snowed in all winter at the station with some macho rednecks. I kept thinking about the older firefighter making comments about my figure and what he'd like to do with me. There was no way I was going to take that job and put myself in a similar position again. I didn't tell people why I turned it down, but I was adamant in my decision.

Instead, I took a job with the state of Arizona doing the same kind of work. It wasn't quite as macho an environment; it was a safer place for me to be. I was doing good natural resource conservation work and still fighting fires. As it turned out, working for a smaller organization meant I was afforded opportunities I would've been passed over for elsewhere. I had no idea at the time, but it would change the trajectory of my career.

Back around 1979, when I had been fighting fires for only five years, there was a fire in the McDowell Mountains, which are now located within the city of Scottsdale and Fountain Hills. In the early 1970s those mountains were my wilderness. There were no homes, no roads, and no people for miles around. Those mountains stood in the wild, overlooking cities that had not yet reached their foothills.

The mountains were my playground from the time I was twelve years old all through high school. Before I could drive, I would beg my mom to let me go camping on my own up there. She would grudgingly drop me off early Saturday morning with the agreement that I'd be back down to the dirt road Sunday afternoon in time for her to pick me up and take me to church for evening mass. I would hike up into the beautiful desert, make camp, hike around, and glory in the beauty of the desert. I learned the names of all the common plants and animals. I bought books about desert wildflowers and took them there with me. I had always loved flowers and plants, and these desert adventures were the beginning of my lifelong study of the natural environment. I spent weekends hiking around, discovering petroglyphs and scouting around old miners' shacks. I watched a pack of coyotes playing together like a bunch of puppies, yipping and jumping around. I was within one hundred feet of them, and though they spotted me, they didn't seem to care.

Once I could drive, I spent many days in my little dune buggy exploring every little canyon with a trail and found even more special places. It was also where I began to understand that the Holy Spirit was alive and well and spoke to my heart. It would be years later when a chief who lived in the Sky City community of the Acoma Pueblo in New Mexico made the connection for me between the Great Spirit and the Holy Spirit. In scripture, God or the Holy Spirit manifests itself within the wilderness, as a burning bush or through the wind. If you think about it, we can't see God—but we can see what God created. By seeing His creation, by living in it and exploring it, I feel an intense spiritual connection. After talking to my priest about it, I came to understand why I felt so close to God when I was in His creation. I became very familiar with those mountains.

The 1979 fire season had been a busy one. The vegetation had grown thick and lush from the winter rains, but now it was June, and the wildflowers and grasses were dried up and ready to burn. This particular June was typical for the Arizona desert, with the high temperatures averaging between 105 to 110 degrees Fahrenheit. It hadn't rained in at least three months. The desert was parched.

A crew of about thirty firefighters had been working its way up the east side of the mountain range. A highly experienced firefighter from the Forest Service regional office in Albuquerque had come to help us. He would be what we used to refer to as the "fire boss" on this fire. From where I sat in the state fire organization at the time, he was a bigwig. I was his second-in-command only because I knew the area so well.

We had been successfully fighting the fire since early in the morning, but it was now around two in the afternoon. The temperature was nearing 107 degrees Fahrenheit, and we were quickly running out of drinking water. With other fires burning around the state, we had no ability to get resupplied by the logistics folks in Phoenix, and we were miles from a road and our vehicles. The fire boss said that we would have to turn around and get more water and come back later in the day. But that would invariably mean that we would lose all the progress we had made on the fire so far. I told him that I thought that there was a spring just on the other side of the ridgetop about a mile or so above us. He looked at me like I was crazy.

"There's no water up here!" he said. "This is June in Phoenix. There's no water in the desert in June around here!"

I told him that I was pretty sure I knew where there was a spring.

In all my years exploring the McDowell Mountains I had never found a spring, but I had seen all the signs that there was one. On the other side of the mountain range from the fire there was an old pipe that had been laid in the bottom of a dry rocky creek, which led down to an old stone cabin and a concrete water trough. I had never seen any water in it, and the pipe was broken in a dozen places. But at some point in time many years ago, someone must have found enough water to fill an old water trough for their livestock.

I didn't give my boss all the details, but I told him that I believed I could find water. He kept insisting that it was a fool's errand and that it would be a waste of time even trying to find water up here. We kept on fighting the fire and working our way higher up the east side of the mountain. Being the stubborn person that I am, I told him that if he let me take four other firefighters all with several one-gallon canteens each, we could bring back twenty gallons of clean cold water for the crew and possibly make it through that day. He must have gotten tired of me nagging him, and I'm sure he thought I was a bit reckless, but he relented. So off we walked, five firefighters carrying four empty one-gallon canteens each, hiking up and over the desert mountains in June.

I wasn't even sure if I was in the right location to go over the mountain pass and find the correct canyon where I had seen that old broken-up water pipe so many years before. But when we made it to the very top of the ridge, I recognized the petroglyphs. I was where I hoped I'd be.

I thought we stood about a half mile above where I thought the spring might be. We hiked down off the ridge into the desert canyon, and sure enough, we found the spring. I saw an old pipe sticking out of a rock with cold, fresh spring water pouring from it and down onto the sandy dry wash below. After about two hours, we returned to the crew with twenty gallons of water. The fire boss thought I had performed a miracle. He was sure he was sending me off on a mission with no chance of success. He was impressed. I didn't think it was anything to make a big deal about. But he did. He kept telling everyone, "Look, look, Scopa found water in a desert."

He told everyone about that event. And from that time on, in his eyes I was golden.

A year later I was on another fire where he was the fire boss. He asked me what my qualifications were. He thought that maybe I had gotten some higher qualifications in the intervening year. I was still just a crew boss, but he gave me a field promotion and made me a sector boss, someone in charge of a small area of the fire. He didn't say it was because I had found water in the desert, but he knew me well enough to know that I could get things done. I had several crews and fire engines working for me. I was successful on the fire, and he continued to think of me positively and treat me like I knew what I was doing. Because of him, I started thinking I knew what I was doing too.

It was the first time in my life that I felt appreciated by someone in a higher level of authority. He recognized my work, thought I did a good job, and rewarded me for that. I didn't feel on edge, worrying about what the boss was thinking or saying about me. It was a new feeling for me.

The next year I found myself on a fire where he was the fire boss once again—but now the nomenclature had changed, and he was the incident commander or "IC." The IC asked me if I had been qualified as a division supervisor yet. Division supervisor was one position above where I had been the year before. I kind of looked at him and shook my head. Inwardly I was laughing. It was just a couple years before when I "found water in the desert" that I was barely a crew boss. And it had only been the previous year that he field-promoted me to sector boss, so there was no way I was qualified as a division supervisor.

The IC made it clear that I should be working as a division supervisor trainee. I had no idea what that entailed, but I was game. It was not like me to say no. I decided I would give it a try, especially since the trainer would be there with me the whole time. I had to take a helicopter ride to find my division. It was way up the mountain from where the incident command post was. There was no way to walk all that way, so I went to the helibase and told them I needed to go to Division Q (my division). There were multiple hotshot crews on my division that would be working for me. When I found my division boss trainer, he briefed me on our objectives, and I began meeting up with all the other resources who would be working for me.

I had quite a shock that afternoon. One of the hotshot crews on the mountain that afternoon had a shock too. The hotshot crew that I had worked for back in 1974 was now working on the division. Many of the same characters who gave me such a hard time were now working for me.

They were incredulous.

"Scopa, how did you get to be the division supervisor?"

I really couldn't tell them at the time. I had no idea myself. But in hindsight I realized I was very fortunate in so many ways. If I hadn't been stubborn and insisted that I could find water, the incident commander would have never promoted me over and over again. That one event, that one fire, set me up to be promoted and be given opportunities that I would never have had otherwise. For years when people asked me how I was promoted so quickly in the wildland fire organizations, I would smile and say because I found water in the desert.

I have to think about all the events that lined up for me to get promoted to division supervisor: My love and spiritual connection to the desert led me to spend so much time in the mountains. I was fortunate to have found the spring that I had never found before. I continued to perform my job well, and I kept running into the same incident commander. Some of my success was due to my ability, but not all. Not all, for sure.

Confidence is critically important when leading firefighters into potentially dangerous situations. It's important that leaders display confidence for those working for them to trust and follow. To some degree, I had been faking my way through life. Pretending to be confident was easy. On another level, I was already confident in my ability to lead firefighters in dangerous situations, but it was critical that my fire boss showed he trusted in my abilities. He played no small part in developing my self-confidence as a leader.

My inner conflict was navigating how to outwardly be confident, leading tough, macho, male firefighters when pretending to be one myself. My old fire boss helped give me the confidence to lead. If he was a well-known, accomplished fire boss and he trusted me, then I must be trustworthy and really know what I'm doing. He was just one of a few others who would help bolster my professional self-esteem.

Opportunities continued to present themselves to me while working for the state. One day my boss came up to me and said, "Scopa, since you're a firefighter and have all that experience with the Forest Service, would you be able to conduct a controlled burn on the Mercer Ranch?"

He way overestimated my experience, but I followed my instinct and lied.

"Sure, I can do that," I said.

I had never conducted a controlled burn. I didn't know the first thing about accomplishing one. When fighting fires, we often have to "burn out" areas to help us contain the fire within our fire lines. I had done a lot of burn-outs in half a dozen fire seasons, and I was an accomplished observer, learning so much in a short time.

A controlled burn is very different than a wildfire. You're applying fire to a landscape with specific goals and objectives. In this case, a rancher wanted to reduce the brush on his state-leased land in order to increase the grasses for his cattle. The controlled burn would not kill the brush, but it would just set it back a bit. It's kind of like trimming the bushes in your yard; they resprout with new green stems. There was likely to be a benefit to the deer and other wildlife in addition to the rancher's cattle. But this was 1979, and I didn't know many people or agencies who were doing much burning in this vegetation type. I would be breaking some new ground—assuming I was successful.

After acting confident with my boss, I drove down to meet with Mr. Mercer to see if I could pull this controlled burn off safely. After looking over the area, and seeing what he wanted to do, I knew his ambitions were bigger than my abilities. I convinced him to scale down the project—instead of burning a few hundred acres on his remote ranch, we agreed to burn three small areas about twenty to forty acres each. We would see how successful we were, and then we could burn some larger areas the next year if it all worked out.

Controlled burns are now referred to as "prescribed burns" because now we write an actual prescription describing how the burn should be conducted and what we're specifically trying to accomplish. Through research studies and experience, we know the best temperatures, relative humidity, wind speed, fuel moistures, and many other parameters necessary to meet the objectives of a burn. In my proposed burn I knew none of that. However, since I was a quick study and had conducted many burn-outs on wildfires, I was confident I could figure out how to safely burn these three small areas. The three areas to be burned were located on a hillside with a sandy, dry wash at the bottom and an old two-track road on the ridgetop. We would be burning between the two.

I gathered up whoever I could find around the office one late spring day and took them with me to conduct the first non-timbered controlled burn for the state agency. Some of my coworkers helping me that day had never even been on a fire before. But they were excited about this adventure, and off we went. I had developed a sound plan in my head and communicated it to everyone involved. Before we lit the match, I made sure everyone had their safety gear on, was briefed, and knew the plan.

We were successful. Three small, controlled burn units were ignited, burned, and safe before we left at the end of the day. It felt good. The three units were monitored for the next few years, and it was determined that the burns did indeed improve the range condition and improve wildlife habitat. The Fish and Game Department, Soil Conservation Service, and the university were all happy. I was too. I felt successful.

Word traveled around the professional circle about my controlled burns in this unique desert scrub ecosystem. I had no idea that it was being spoken about, but apparently word had spread. I started getting phone calls from other agencies in the Southwest asking for my "prescriptions." I kept referring those who called to a national research station who were and should be the experts on this sort of thing. When one of the callers told me that they had already called the research station and the research station referred them to me, I just laughed. I should have written up my results and had them published, but at the time I was just stumbling through life and grateful for the small wins I had been blessed with.

Yet amid all my successes on the outside, within a year of my wedding and starting my job for the state of Arizona, my outer fabric was beginning to show signs of wear and tear. If you looked closely, you might see something that was supposed to be hidden. I was developing anxiety about how I would continue. I was struggling to hold it together. I knew I just had to try and bring the subject up with my wife.

We were out on a date, enjoying a warm spring evening, and I said I had something important to tell her. She said she did too. I told her to go first with what she wanted to talk about because I knew my topic would be depressing and disheartening.

She announced that it was time to have a baby. My heart at once soared and sunk. I desperately wanted a baby. I wanted children around the house. I was the favorite uncle; my little nephews and nieces swarmed me when I was around. Now I would have a child of my own. I hugged her and said yes. I wanted to have a baby with her. I was excited and confused. How would this work? How was I going to continue? Did I have the strength to keep up the act? My outer fabric was already fraying. Could I keep it together so no one could see the real me? She asked me what I had wanted to talk about, but I just said, "Nothing important." After the news of her wanting to start a family, I was torn, not knowing what to do or what to say. I smiled and thanked God I would be a parent with all the blessings and heartaches.

A common refrain came to mind. A refrain that I would have to tell myself many times every day over the next fifteen years.

"Suck it up, Scopa. You've got to suck it up."

I had to be tougher than my gender identity. I knew I could be, but I had to figure out how. I had to come up with a new coping mechanism. What might help? How was I going to make it through for my children? I was grasping at straws. The only thing that had helped in the past was further wrapping myself in a thicker, tougher covering, and firefighting was what I knew. Flawed reasoning, I know. Firefighting wasn't only a good cover for me; it also provided an effective distraction. When you're busy learning new skills, you have less time to think about your problems. And the excitement of emergency calls can almost be like a drug. Instead of using alcohol or other substances, the adrenaline provided assistance in coping with my life's big challenge.

One idea was to quit working for the state natural resource agency. Although the work was good and I loved caring for our environment, I was going to have to do something else to survive. I decided I was going to have to do something more masculine. If I wrapped myself in something more dangerous, more courageous, more manly, that would make me tougher, that would keep the woman inside me at bay.

I had an opportunity to test for and become a full-time city fire-fighter. Surely that would do it. It would be how I would survive. A new job like this would give me more cover. It wasn't going to fix me; there wasn't any long-term fix that I could see. I was just hoping for a solution that would help for the next few years. If it weren't so tragic, it would be comical. The worse my psyche was becoming, the more I tried to hide behind the macho uniform of a firefighter. I tested and was hired.

I was now a full-time city firefighter. I could get caught up in the excitement, the newness, the danger—and it was easier to hide from myself. My gender identity was still on my mind every minute of the day, but at least there were distractions. And the distractions were fun: going on fires, responding to auto accidents, medical calls, climbing a cliff to save an injured rock climber, hazardous materials calls. I was saving lives. It was exciting. But even though I was hiding me from me,

I wasn't doing a good a job of hiding me from those around me. I was as deep undercover as I could get, yet every once in a while, someone saw through my disguise, and I freaked out.

In the morning at work, our routine after the regular daily chores was for one of the apparatuses (fire engine or rescue truck) to make a grocery run for the day. The firefighters worked at the fire station for twenty-four hours, and it was considered part of the daily regimen. We did this within our "first due" area—the area surrounding the station, where an engine responds—and we were always available to respond as well. One day, we were at the local grocery store near the fire station, about to push our cart into the checkout line. Three of us were standing relatively near each other when a gentleman in his sixties elbowed one of my coworkers, pointed at me, and said, "When did you guys start hiring women?"

My coworkers laughed. I walked away, pretending I wasn't bothered. I was doing the best imitation of a man that I could do. This was it! I had regulation short hair, and I was in uniform. If my figure wasn't that of a typical guy, I had no control over that. But this was as good as it was going to get.

I was angry. It was like some old random guy saw through my outer fabric, and I felt naked, seen. The guys just thought it was funny and nothing else was said, but it affected me. Over the years I had many similar experiences. I don't know if it was because I was short or if it was my shape. But when it happened, it was disorienting. What were they seeing? What was it that they saw?

Since high school, I had to buy men's pants a couple sizes too large in order to fit my hips. I became very adept at taking in the waist to make the pants fit. I could split the rear seam, take off the belt loop, sew the waist back smaller, put the belt loop back on, and I'd be good to go. It was routine. There were very few pants that I owned that didn't require that alteration. When I was busy, I sometimes would just purchase women's jeans, so I didn't have to take them apart and make the alteration. But I still thought my cover was working.

Considering everything that was going on, life was good. My wife had a good job and was quite successful. The kids were healthy and doing well in school. I was a captain at the fire department. My marriage was pretty good, as long as I didn't try to talk about important things such as who I was. I didn't know how long I would be able to keep up the walls, the defenses. The fabric, with all my alterations, was holding together for now, even if it was slowly wearing out.

6

HOLDING ON
FOR DEAR LIFE

To PUT IT MILDLY, MY life was complicated. I loved some parts of it and
was terrified by other parts. Life can be weird that way. Certain parts of
my job were awesome. Most of my time on the fire department, I worked
with some great guys and felt like a member of the team. When I was
promoted to captain, I had a regular set of employees working for me
day after day. We became close, like family.

Yet I found out that when a firefighter was getting transferred to
my shift, often they weren't happy about it. My reputation was great
among my coworkers. They knew I did a decent job, that I was a good
captain, so that wasn't it. But I was suspicious in the eyes of most of the
fire department members. It's not even clear to me all these years later
why I was suspect. I just wasn't one of the cool kids. Was it related to
people thinking I wasn't macho enough? Did the chip on my shoulder
get in the way? I'm not sure. Could they see through my outer fabric? I
think that was a part of it. Years later, I learned that my college degree
added to their wariness about me. Back when I started as a firefighter,
a four-year degree wasn't very common in the fire department. I would
go on to get most of another, as well as a master's degree. I would really
be suspicious then.

I don't know how much of the difficulty had to do with other people's assumptions or suspicions that I was different, and how much was me. The fact is, because I was always trying to prove myself, I might have acted like a jerk at times. I was always on guard trying to protect my identity, not letting too much of my true self show through the fabric. I thought I was acting like a normal guy, friendly and easygoing.

When personnel were transferred to my shift and we began working and living together for twenty-four-hour shifts, we almost always became close friends or at least respected coworkers.

At night in the bunkroom with the lights out and the guys talking for a bit before falling asleep, I felt like a spy amid the enemy. It's not like I thought the guys were the enemy at all. But for them, the firehouse was a safe space to open up. They spoke often about their feelings about their wives and kids and relationships. From my perspective, they were an odd group. I didn't understand them. It hadn't yet occurred to me that men and women often think differently and can have vastly different perspectives. And I didn't realize that I thought like a woman. Listening in to their conversations at night in a dark fire station bunkroom, I felt like I caught a glimpse into what guys really think about and how they feel. I felt like an undercover agent.

At some point, someone told me about the book *Men Are from Mars, Women Are from Venus* written by John Gray. When I read the book, I thought I had found the Holy Grail of interpretation. This was big! It was as though I had found the key to understanding my peers, or had woken up one day fluent in a foreign language. For me, this book was critical to understanding some of the difficulties I had at work. Back then I hadn't yet adapted, and my communication style was not the direct style that the guys responded to.

After a fire or a drill when we used air bottles for our self-contained breathing apparatuses, those bottles had to be refilled from our in-station system. It wasn't a lot of work, but it took some time. The empty bottles were stacked in an assigned location, and then after being filled they were laid down in another location. Once all the bottles were filled, they were moved once again into the racks to be put back on the engines when needed. Sometimes the bottles sat on the ground when they should have been put up into the racks on the wall. Firefighters shouldn't have to be told to put the filled bottles up in the racks. They know.

One day as captain, I was working in my office while the crew was finishing some chores around the station. It was mid-morning, and when I saw some bottles lying on the ground I mentioned to the crew, "Hey, those bottles are on the ground."

I received the normal grunt of affirmation to my comment.

After lunch I walked by the compressor and saw the bottles still on the ground. Once again, I said a little more clearly, "Guys, those bottles are on the still on the ground."

After returning from a call later that afternoon, I noticed the bottles still in the same location. I thought I was going to lose it! I was so mad I couldn't stand it. I felt my crew was disrespecting me. I would not stand for it.

I had a bit of a meltdown and yelled at them, "How many times do I have to tell you? Put those damned bottles up in the racks. I asked you twice already, and they're still on the ground."

My good, hardworking, mostly well-intentioned firefighters looked like they just got in trouble with Mom. "Gosh, you never told us to put the bottles up. If you wanted them put up, why didn't you say something?"

"Take some deep breaths, Scopa, breathe deep," I said to myself. Sometimes I just had to wonder.

Dr. Gray's book helped me realize that I wasn't using the guys' communication style. If my boss had said the same thing to me about the bottles, I would have known that their intent was for me to put the bottles up in the racks. I'm not suggesting that communication between the genders is a simple thing to learn from a quick read, but the book did open my eyes to the fact that maybe my gender issues were affecting more than just my internal thinking. I realized that my communication style and other traits that were often coded as "feminine" were even more hardwired than I thought. All my trying to act masculine had somehow convinced me that I *was* masculine. If I acted masculine, then I must be. But when things like this happened, I was reminded that I really was faking it and had to adapt.

Even with all my struggles, I generally built good relationships with the guys I worked with. When it was duck-hunting season, I knew many of the areas out in the wilds of Arizona, so I was a source of information for my coworkers on possible hunting locations. There were days when our crew all went together to get a few ducks. I wasn't much of a hunter; it was more a social activity for me. We were not always successful, but after spending twenty-four hours together at work, we still enjoyed each other's company enough to cram into a truck together and bounce around some old ranch roads in search of ducks on a faraway pond.

We'd often travel together to go skiing on a day off. My wife drove a big Chevy Suburban, and I'd borrow it for the day while she was working. We'd load everyone up, including my two kids whom I regularly took out of school to go skiing, and B-Shift from Station 1 would have a ski day. I cherish those memories because now, very few of my old coworkers will really have much to do with me. That's how the equation gets balanced in the long run: can't have too much good.

But for a while the good outweighed the bad. On a day when we responded to a call for a possible diabetic emergency, we arrived to find an elderly man in bed thrashing about and cussing like a drunken sailor. His poor wife was so embarrassed by his language that she was fretting and apologizing to us. We had a pretty good idea that if we could start an IV with glucose, he'd calm right down in a minute or so.

He was so combative we couldn't get the IV in. One of the guys said to me, "Get up on his chest and hold him still."

I was pretty slim, and I was definitely the smallest one on the fire engine and medic unit. So, there on his bed, I climbed on top of him and straddled his chest with my legs to hold him down. I had his torso and one arm held down, and the guys held his other arm trying to get the IV started. During this whole adventure, he called us every name in the book while cursing at us to send us "all to hell." His poor wife was afraid and embarrassed. But once the IV was in, he started to quiet down. Finally, he looked up at me with crystal-clear eyes and politely asked, "Excuse me, but would you mind getting off my chest?"

I smiled and said, "Of course, pardon me."

He was transported to the hospital and had his medicine adjusted and was fine, at least for now. It was a typical medical call. Nothing out of the ordinary. But I felt a camaraderie and a kinship with my crew. That was how I survived.

There was another firefighter whom I had worked with before on another crew. When I got promoted to captain, he came to work on my engine as the firefighter-medic along with another two firefighters. He had two young children, and our families became friends. Our families would join us for Thanksgiving or Christmas dinner, or someone's birthday, at the fire station. We had to work regardless, so our families would come to the station, and we'd have everything cleaned up with extra tables and chairs for the event. The kids loved it, and it made being away from home during the holidays tolerable. Over time, you'd get to know everyone's kids and spouses. When he and his wife were going to have their newest baby christened, they asked me to be the godfather. I was honored to be asked—and felt more pressure. Years later, like most of my friends and coworkers from those old days, he doesn't talk to me anymore. But in that moment, I was surviving.

Those simple moments, along with the ski trips and hunting trips, made me feel like I was a normal person, like I belonged and could make this last. But even with all the friendship and camaraderie, I was ill at ease because I could feel the strain on the fabric. The real me under my fabric covering was showing more and more.

I never knew what people could see or what they thought of me. I didn't really want to know. While working one evening at the fire station, one of my coworkers and I were talking. Somehow the topic of what people thought of me came up. I didn't want to hear anything about it.

But my friend said, "You know what people think? You know what they say?"

"Stop," I said. "I don't want to know. Don't say anything else." *What would I do with that information?* I thought.

We had free beer at our firefighter's union meetings. It was a way to encourage attendance at the meetings. No one drank very much, but there was always a cooler, and the firefighters would have a beer or two during the meeting. Once while attending a meeting, I got up to get a beer and turned around to ask the guys next to me if I could grab them one while I was up. Some firefighters behind me from another station mumbled under their breath but loud enough for me and those around them to hear, "Why don't you just wear a dress?"

I never paused or acknowledged the comment. I brought back a couple beers for my friends and ignored the jerks sitting behind me. What were they seeing? Was it feminine to ask if my friends wanted a beer while I was up? I never understood those kinds of comments and attitudes, but I knew very clearly: I was not one of the guys.

I had my struggles at home too. Raising two children and being married was everything to me. With my firefighter's schedule, I was home twenty days a month. That left me time to volunteer at the kids' school and gave me the opportunity to be more involved than most parents. I did the shopping, laundry, and kept up the house. Those minor domestic chores gave me a sense of normalcy. When my next-door neighbor would see me hanging up the laundry on the backyard clothesline, he'd yell, "Hey Hazel, I need my laundry done too."

I ran a small land-management consulting business that augmented my firefighter's salary and only required a couple days a month of my time. At home I didn't have the distractions that work afforded me, but there were positive trade-offs. The kids were in school, my wife was at work, and I was happy to be taking are of the home front's domestic chores of shopping, cooking, and cleaning. Our marriage was not seen as traditional by my coworkers. I was suspect. There were snide comments made by firefighters from other stations about me and my relationship with my wife. She was guilty by association with me.

I was in my midthirties when I started having some strange reactions to seeing a newborn child or a mom with a newborn. I had two amazing children whom I loved with all my heart. But I began to have such an ache when I saw a baby with their mom. It was strong enough to bring tears to my eyes. The emotion was unclear to me. All I knew was I felt a longing and an emptiness when I witnessed the maternal scene. It would be years later, describing those feelings of loss and emptiness in therapy, when it became clear to me. I was experiencing the need to bear a child. It never made sense to me since I was raising my own two children, but it wasn't the same. I might have been feeding babies and changing diapers and waking up in the middle of the night with every known issue, but it wasn't the same. I didn't know why at the time, but I cried over the feeling and the need to have a child.

Again, I tried to bring up the topic of being transgender to my wife. Over the years, if she had been drinking, I could bring up the topic, and she would talk about it freely. She was more open to hearing my troubles if she'd had a drink to relax her. When I was able to have a frank discussion with her about my pain and struggles, I was elated. I thought my troubles would be lessened. Just having my loving partner to talk to about it would be a huge help.

But on the mornings after our discussions, it was like nothing had ever been said. She claimed to never remember our conversations. I expected too much from her. I had put her on a pedestal in my mind's eye, and I never recognized her fears, issues, and insecurities. I was so blinded by my own insecurities, I didn't realize she had her own too. She was in the car with me on that fog-shrouded highway driving way too fast. But she just told me to keep driving, don't look, don't talk, just drive.

My decision to not make *any* decision was getting more and more costly.

7

THE UNRAVELING

As TIME WENT BY AND my children were growing up, my wife became tired of my gender struggles. My decades-long personal battles were wearing on her too. My outer fabric was ripping, and it was getting hard to hide who I was—to keep pretending to be someone I wasn't.

Have you ever had to hold a position in a school play without moving? Or maybe you were in the military and had to stand at attention for a long time. At some point, your muscles need to move, to relax, to flex in another position. You need to shake your limbs and move your head around to keep from cramping up. For me, I got to the point that I didn't know how to stand anymore. I mean literally: I didn't know how to stand anymore. Every time I went to sit, stand, or walk, I was constantly consciously aware of how I was holding my body—and how it might look to everyone around me. I had spent so much time and energy in my thirty-five-year life thinking about how to stand, how to walk, and how to talk that it was making me crazy. All my energy had been going in to making sure I was acting like a man so no one could see the real me inside. I got to the point that I didn't know how to stand or walk or talk anymore.

I was getting close to my breaking point. I became quiet and depressed. I didn't know how much longer I was going to survive. I had used up all the distractions I could think of. I had been decorated with awards and medals for heroism and performance as a firefighter. I had volunteered to be on the hazardous materials team and was a member of the high-angle special rescue unit. The hazmat team responds to chemical spills, gas leaks, or any emergency that requires special training and equipment. We detected, contained, and removed hazardous substances from the scene. The high-angle special rescue crew responds to emergencies that also require special training and equipment. In my case, it was almost always a mountain rescue: someone injured on a cliff or mountain, which required us to transport using ropes or involved rappelling.

These were distractions and camouflage that I thought would help keep me a man. But it was a ridiculous concept, like trying to stand in the middle of a swift-moving river and insist that I can walk against the current. You might hold up for a while, but eventually you'll be washed downstream. The inevitability of it was absolute, but still I resisted.

My wife's career was important to her, and her potential for promotions was almost limitless. She was very intelligent and capable, and she had always made more money than I had. For years she had been encouraged by her supervisors to move and start promoting up through the system. It was me and my career that were holding her back.

Working at the fire department was supposed to help me cope. It was supposed to help me stay a man. It was supposed to be a framework of masculinity that would keep me from collapsing into the woman I was inside. But that was always a flawed strategy. It was based on bad and incomplete information.

Eventually, my wife and I thought a change of scenery would be good for us. She would take a promotion on the East Coast and start moving up in her career, and I would leave the fire department, which would, I hoped, alleviate some of my gender discomfort. Maybe being away from the macho work environment would make things easier on me. There would be less pressure, and I wouldn't be so stressed. I thought if I could just find some calm water I could continue to tread, keep my head above the surface, and survive.

The next few years were tumultuous. I finished my master's degree, and my wife focused on her new job. My children were growing up to be truly amazing people. Smart, hardworking, and with so much potential. But watching them grow up was scary too.

When my children were very young, I was just Dad. They had no concept of my struggles; their perception of me was as their hero. They knew of my awards, pictures in the newspaper, and the work I did as a firefighter. When my fire engine was driving near their school and I knew it was time for their recess, I'd have the driver steer the fire engine down the street next to the school playground. The driver would blow the airhorn as we drove by the schoolyard, and all the kids would scream and wave. That's who I was in my children's eyes: the brave hero firefighter. But even then, I knew that it would be different as the kids got older and they started to see me like others did. I would be the weird dad their friends made fun of. I knew that was going to happen, and it hurt so badly.

I often volunteered at school because my work schedule allowed it. I was the parent who instigated ski trips and camping trips or sailing for a week at a time. I rarely did anything that didn't involve my children, and our relationship reflected that bond.

When I left the fire department and we moved, I started graduate school. I let my hair grow out. It was a visible outward sign of who I was becoming. In some ways, that's all it took. With my now long hair, I was mistaken for a woman almost every day. While at the plant nursery with my kids and wearing blue jeans, a sweatshirt, and baseball cap, an employee addressed me as "ma'am."

One time the gutters needed replacing on our house. I called to get a bid. But when the owner of the company arrived, he said, "I'm sorry, ma'am, but I really can't give you a bid unless your husband is here to talk to." I wasn't trying to present as a woman—I had just stopped making a concerted effort to appear as a man.

Even after I left the fire department, I was still able to keep fighting fires. During the summertime there are opportunities for those with fire qualifications to be hired as a "casual" temporary employee and work on a wildfire. My qualifications were solid, and I had all my paperwork ready to go. When I got a call from one of the wildland fire agencies in Arizona to see if I was available to come out for a month or so to help work on some fires, I took the offer and went back west. My wife and I had been struggling at home, this opportunity would pay well, and I'd get into some familiar territory. I missed fighting fires, and regardless of gender, it was fun. So off I went for most of the summer.

During one fire in Oregon that year, I was assigned as a division supervisor on a very large forest fire. It was busy, I was given great assignments, and I had a great supervisor. But for the team managing the fire, having someone like me come in is always challenging. Here is someone who's a temporary employee from another part of the country. I didn't have a truck since I'd been flown in, so I was assigned a local driver with a pickup to be my transportation for the next few weeks.

One day I was told that I would be moved forward on the fire, which meant that as the fire was moving across the mountains, I would be moving with it and would take over supervision on that part of the fire. I knew it meant that my supervisor trusted my work and he was rewarding me with a good assignment. In order to come up with a plan to put in our fire lines, I was told to go to the helibase and take a reconnaissance flight to become familiar with the area.

Off I went with the driver to the helibase. When we got to the helibase, the security guard was at the bottom of the hill, stopping traffic to make sure that anyone entering the base had legitimate business there. I told him that the operations chief had told me to get a flight of my new division. I don't think the security guard was too familiar with fire operations, and he just looked at me with a blank stare.

"I'm a division supervisor, and I need to take a flight," I said.

He wasn't getting it.

"Hey, I've got some woman in a truck down here who says she's supposed to take a helicopter ride," I overheard him say into the radio.

My driver absolutely knew that I was a guy. I wasn't trying to pass myself off as a woman, and this security guard was really making me angry. My driver started to laugh at the situation. I wasn't laughing. I looked at her and said, "Drive," meaning for her to just drive on past the checkpoint and on up to the helibase.

The security guard said, "You can't go up there! You can't go up there!" I looked the driver square in the eye and said, "Drive this damned truck! NOW!"

Off she drove past the security guard and past the checkpoint. I got my flight, and all was well. But it was a realization for me just how I was perceived. It's a precarious place to be in the fire service. A guy who isn't masculine? That's dangerous ground.

A couple weeks later it was mid-September in the high country of eastern Oregon, and it was getting cold. At this point the management team on the fire had combined multiple divisions and made them all into one. So now I was supervising dozens of small fire engines and many twenty-person hand crews spread over five or six miles. I had been having fun. It was a good fire, which for me meant that I had plenty of firefighters, fire trucks, bulldozers, and equipment to get the job done well. A good fire is an active, busy fire, and it was so good to be back on the ground doing what I loved.

It was below freezing when we woke up, and cold all morning. The firefighters would be moving slowly from the cold. I directed my driver to go to the kitchen while I was in the morning briefing and get some insulated containers of hot coffee. The kitchen had five-gallon containers made just for this purpose. While I was making the rounds checking in with those supervisors who were working for me on the line, the firefighters could take a break and get a hot cup of coffee. Their boss and I talked about the daily progress and possible problems.

As I got out of the truck at one of the drop points to speak with one of my strike team leaders, a big bubba redneck firefighter walked toward me. I told him there was hot coffee in the truck and then asked him where his strike team leader was.

Instead of answering my question, he asked, "Are you girls from the kitchen?" He put his arm around my shoulder and said again, "You girls from the kitchen? You brought us coffee? How sweet."

I couldn't decide if I was angry or if I should be laughing. What an idiot! So I thought I'd have some fun with the guy.

"No, asshole," I said. "I'm your division supervisor. Now where's your strike team leader?"

He scrambled away, apologizing as he went. All this time on the fire, I was wearing my protective Nomex firefighter clothing, boots, helmet, and my pack—but this is what happens when you're living in between genders.

Away from the strict, daily confines of masculinity in the fire department, life wasn't so bad, as people saw "me," but at the same time it was also bad, very bad. Back home, the kids seemed to ignore when these things happened around them—or at least they never said anything to me. But I know my son was teased by his school friends because of me. More than once, a teacher or friend would say to him "Your mom is here" when I would come pick him up from a school activity, while wearing jeans and T-shirts.

When it happened around my wife, I knew I was in trouble.

While visiting Memphis for our twentieth wedding anniversary, we were having a burger and beer on Beale Street and looking forward to listening to some good music. I had made a special effort that night to do my best imitation of a guy: a pair of khaki slacks, a golf shirt, and my hair in a ponytail. Two guys sitting at the next table offered to buy us drinks. One of them pointed to me and asked my wife, "What's she drinking?" I knew the rest of the evening was going to be bad, and it was.

Whenever this happened around her, she would become enraged with me. But on that night, when these guys were clearly trying to flirt with both of us by buying us drinks, the tension was worse than normal.

My wife was OK with my gender struggles—as long as no one else knew. But when two guys offered to buy us drinks, that was it. It was now becoming difficult to pass as a man. We had started going to marriage counseling together. After a couple of months, she decided she didn't want to go anymore. She told the therapist that the problem was mine, not hers, and quit going. I continued to go, becoming more withdrawn within my marriage and my life. I felt quiet and depressed, and on the advice of my therapist I started taking antidepressants.

Months later, I had to drive across the country for some business that would take me back to Arizona. I would be staying with my parents, but I had a long two-day drive to get there. I pulled into a truck stop to get gas in Oklahoma and figured I should use the restroom while I was there. Wearing my regular jeans, a ranch jacket, and western boots, I walked into the men's restroom.

Immediately a man in the restroom anxiously said, "Ma'am, ma'am, you're in the wrong restroom. This is the men's restroom."

My eyes opened wide. Not knowing what to say or what to do, I turned around and walked out.

I went outside into the cold Oklahoma wind and got back into my truck. I still had to pee, but what was I supposed to do? I sat down in my truck, shaken up, not knowing what to do. I pulled back onto the freeway and drove on, wondering all the while. Between my fragile emotional state and being told I was in the wrong restroom, I started to cry. How was I going to go on? The question applied not just to my trip, but to my life.

I decided I had to pee, and if I couldn't use the men's restroom, I'd use the women's. At the next truck stop, I pulled in and walked into the women's restroom. I was scared, but I had to use someone's restroom. And at this point, I didn't care whose it was. I bought some lipstick, and for the rest of the trip I used the women's bathrooms.

After completing my master's degree, I hadn't found a job yet. A local department store was hiring for the holidays, and I thought I could at least take a temporary position to help with some household income. During orientation the supervisor explained that the company had a strict dress code: men had to wear ties, and women had to wear nice slacks and a blouse or a dress. I was shocked. In my state of mind, I couldn't stand the thought of wearing a tie. It would be like dressing in drag. I might not be trying to pass as a woman, but a tie, I was going to have to wear a tie? The thought depressed me. I wouldn't do it. I couldn't do it.

On my first day of work, I wore slacks and a nice sweater. I reasoned that the manager might assume I had a shirt and tie on under my sweater. I was surprised when a customer referred to me as "Miss Bobbie." Oh, so that was it. I didn't have to wear a tie. I continued working for the holiday season wearing my slacks and sweaters and made it through never having to wear a tie. My understanding of where I fell on the gender continuum was skewed. I hadn't yet realized how feminine I already was. But the fear of losing everything in my life outweighed any happiness that I might have felt when I was referred to as "miss" or "ma'am." The inevitability that my wife and family would leave if I either transitioned or continued in my androgynous middle ground was like a boulder hanging over my head ready to crush me. I was growing emotionally brittle—and I was becoming more depressed.

The stress I was under felt suffocating. I had turned to therapy, antidepressants, reading scripture, and praying like a warrior to cope. I knew I was near the end of my wife's patience with dealing with my depression and the pressures that my gender identity was putting on the family. I had always known that God created me this way. It wasn't due to some type of family dysfunction that messed up my psyche and emotional health. I never doubted that, but now I was willing to try anything, and since my faith tradition was Christian, I went to church for a "healing."

I was asking for a healing, but what I really wanted was a cure. Like many Christians, I had confused the two. A healing would come, but a cure was not in the celestial cards.

When I explained my problem to those who were going to pray over me for the healing, they said, "You have a demon inside you. Open your eyes and let the power of Jesus Christ cast out the demon."

I'll admit, I didn't have a lot of faith in the exercise. I had been praying to God my entire life. I had more emotion and desire and faith for a healing than these strangers could possibly muster, but I was willing to try. I just wanted to be a normal human being. I would pray with them with my eyes open and ask Jesus to heal me. Hands were laid on me, and the prayers began. I prayed.

It felt a bit disrespectful on their part. I mean, was I supposed to have been walking around with a demon inside of me since I was four years old? How did the demon survive in me through all my prayers and reading of scripture? It seemed a bit odd, but I was willing to try, and I gave it my all. After a while, they were done. Unsurprisingly, no demon was expelled, and I had to deal with my challenge on my own with the gifts God had already given me. In all fairness to those praying over me, I doubt they even knew what being transgender meant and what they were really praying for. I kept stumbling on.

For some trans people, the thought of beginning hormone therapy is a dream. It can be seen as a panacea to the problems of life. In a moment of desperation and stupidity, I requested that my doctor prescribe me a low dose of female hormone medication. In hindsight, it made little sense for me. I knew my marriage was ending. My wife repeatedly told me that she wasn't divorcing me *today*. So I knew the end was right around the corner. The desperation came from the depression of losing my wife and family. It came from not knowing where to turn. The desperation was deep in my soul. And for some reason, hormone therapy sounded like a possible solution.

With severe depression and desperation in my heart, I thought that maybe a low dose of estrogen medicine couldn't hurt. Maybe it would even help me. I was under a doctor's care, and he thought it would be safe since it was such a low dose. It would be so slight that I would see no effect at all. Unfortunately, that turned out to be untrue.

Just going to a gender specialist caused changes. Before the doctor prescribed any medication, he insisted on a physical exam to make sure I was healthy. As part of the examination, he examined my genital area. He looked up at me and asked, "How old were you when you were injured?"

"What?" I replied.

"You were obviously hurt when you were young. You're not properly developed."

I was stunned. How could I be forty years old and not know I hadn't developed correctly? My head was spinning. I knew I was very small down there, but what?

"Wait a minute, what are you saying?" I asked.

The doctor described that it appeared that either I had been injured in my genital area when I was still young and growing or, possibly, that I had had surgery on my genitals when I was very young. I didn't know what to say. No one had ever mentioned anything to me. And I had fathered two children, so I know things weren't completely messed up. I was confused and in shock. I didn't know what to say.

He went on to say he could prescribe a very low dose of estrogen medication. He advised me that because it was at such a low dose, I wouldn't see any physical effects for months or even longer, but it might offer some emotional calming. I had read that some transgender people feel some emotional relief from a low dose of estrogen. The doctor said if I wanted to transition, I would need a much higher dose of estrogen to counteract the effects of my naturally produced testosterone. I assured him that I did not want to transition.

Maybe his advice was good and accurate for ninety-nine percent of his patients. It turned out not to be accurate for me.

After two weeks I decided that I was playing with fire. In my mind, taking estrogen—any dosage of estrogen—meant that I was going to pursue transitioning, that I'd somehow already decided. My priority was to stay married and with my family, and one was not possible with the other. I thought that maybe there was still some hope that I could maintain my marriage, so I threw out the medication that I had just started and had spent so much time thinking about. I knew I had to just hold on a little bit longer.

But shortly after throwing the medicine into the trash, I started noticing a difference. My breasts became tender. Then they started to leak. On several occasions, I lost track of several hours of time. I was sitting down at a desk, and when I looked up at the clock, three hours had gone by. I was in a daze, yet I hadn't been taking the medication for weeks. I was getting chills at odd times. When I went to donate blood, like I did on a regular basis, I was turned away because my iron level was too low. I went back to my regular doctor, who confirmed my iron was indeed too low. They said, "Come back in a week and we'll test it again." When I went back to have blood tested, my iron count was too high. The doctor said to quit taking iron supplements. But I wasn't taking any iron supplements. Something was wrong.

I went back to the gender specialist to find out what was going on.

"You might be having some issues unrelated to the estrogen therapy," he told me.

I told him that I had thrown out the medicine a month ago.

He looked at my chart, puzzled. "Well, this is odd," he said.

My blood work showed unusually high estrogen levels.

"Your estrogen should have never gone up this high on the dose you were taking," he said. "Let's wait a few weeks, and we'll take some more blood and see. Your blood estrogen level should go back down."

It didn't go back down. My estrogen levels continued to rise. Apparently, the reason for my elevated blood estrogen levels could be a pituitary tumor or something similar. I continued to get my blood tested, and after about six months my estrogen levels finally tapered off but never went back to normal. When the test results for tumors came back negative, the doctor was perplexed. He suggested that I possibly had some ovarian tissue in my body that would produce estrogen and that could explain a lot of my problems. It didn't explain anything for me, but the mystery would have to be dealt with sometime in the future. For now, I was an emotional wreck. Trying the low-dose estrogen only made my life worse.

Twenty-five years have gone by since those heartbreaking days, and my hormones have continued to go up and down throughout these years. What's more, I notice when they do. They cycle about every three or four months, and at the age of sixty-five, without any estrogen therapy in many years, I can still tell when my estrogen level is elevated. I've been to some excellent doctors at the best medical centers. But it's one of life's mysteries that I just gave up hoping to answer.

After years of marital struggles, in 1997 my wife told me she wanted a divorce. She refused to help me tell the kids why we were divorcing. She said it was my issue and my responsibility to tell them. My son was fourteen at the time.

I sat on the big living room chair next to a big window looking at the big oak trees in our backyard and explained to him that because of my gender struggles, his mom and I couldn't stay together. As he laid across my lap hugging me and crying, he said, "I don't care about that. I just don't want you to go."

My heart was broken, and it has never ever healed from that one moment so many years ago. The image of my skinny little buddy lying across my lap crying has been chiseled into the stone of my soul. Of course, I didn't want to go either. I never wanted to leave my children, but I felt so guilty that I grudgingly went along with my wife's demands and left the family. It was a mistake and a regret that I will take to my grave.

Telling my seventeen-year-old daughter was very different, but equally painful. We went to a local park to have the dreaded discussion.

When I told her about the upcoming divorce, she was silent and angry at me. Her good life up to that point was going to change drastically. She had every right to be mad at me. But her only comment was, "How could you not tell me about this for all these years?"

My daughter wanted to know why I hadn't told her the biggest secret in the Scopa family for the last forty years.

Why hadn't I told her? It was a good question. Why couldn't I have told her? We had been very close while she was growing up. I was very involved in her life. She was always open with me, and I valued our special relationship. But in my life and with my family, we could never talk about this. You don't speak about it. You pretend, you try to protect those around you, you buck up, and you move on. God forbid, you don't talk about the hurt and the shame.

My children's lives were torn apart, never to be the same. Everything they thought they had and knew about me and our family was now gone. In their mind—and because of what everyone in my family had told them—they no longer had a father. Their dad didn't exist any longer. All their hurt and fear and anger was on me. And I bought into it. I accepted fault for everything because that was all I knew. I tried to assert myself as their dad, but it was clear: no one other than me thought I was.

I lost everything in the divorce. In my state of mind, I thought that was only fair. My good Catholic guilt overrode my intelligence and objectivity. My soon-to-be ex was worried that the kids would want to live with me rather than her. Because of my past work schedule, the time I spent with them, and our personalities, I had been at least as involved if not more so in our children's lives. I don't mean to say she wasn't a loving parent—she loved our children without question, and she was a great mom. But due to her own insecurities and because of my love and involvement in my kids' lives, she worried that they'd want to go with me after the divorce. I had always been the fun parent. I was the social director. I organized the family trips. I took them skiing. I took them boating. I was the parent in their classroom. I was the parent who picked them up from school. But she made it clear: "You will not get the kids." And rather than fight to remain in their lives, I accepted her demands and went away. It was a huge mistake on my part.

I had no income after the divorce, so I had no way to care for the kids even if they had wanted to come with me. The great tragedy of my life was the loss of my children. I was devastated. My children had been my entire life; they were what gave my struggle purpose. My life had been revolving around my kids for the last seventeen years. They had made it possible for me to go on as long as I had.

I think it's predictable yet reductive that a transgender person might seem self-absorbed and selfish to their family and friends around them when they transition. All the bystanders know is that all of a sudden, Bobbie is leaving the family to "live his life." "How selfish!" they say. "How could he do that to his kids?" I didn't have the tools, the knowledge, to fight back. I had no support from my family. They had completely sided with my wife. My kids were old enough to decide who they wanted to live with or if they even wanted to visit, and had I tried to push it; in 1997 no judge would have sided with me. It all added to my feelings of being defeated. I felt like my body had joined forces with my family. I was not going to win. So I left in defeat.

The choice was to lose my family or lose my life. It was that simple and that clear. It was never selfish.

I constantly worried about how to protect my kids. How do I do everything I can to help them in life? Would my children be better off with their dad as a woman, or would they be better off with the memory of a dead hero-firefighter dad? This was the literal conversation going on in my mind. I spent hours, day after day, praying to God for help. I knew suicide was wrong, but what if I killed myself to protect my children? Surely God would understand if I killed myself to save my kids! What parent wouldn't die to save their children?

There were long, tearful prayers and conversations with God in those days. How do I decide what is the best choice for my kids? If I had been able to stay male for another few years, until they were both out of college, then that would have been the plan. But I couldn't do it; it wasn't an option. The fabric was so torn it was just remnants and scraps. I was out of cover. I was at the end. I thought about ways to end my life that would appear like an accident so the kids wouldn't have to deal with the impacts of a parent committing suicide. But after a year of prayer and deep soul-searching, life won out. For better or worse, I decided to live, and I believed they would eventually rather have me alive than an image of who they thought their dad was.

I hope most parents don't ever to have to struggle with those same questions. But after years of therapy and no family support, at forty years of age, I knew I was either going to survive as a woman *or I would not survive.* My core identity was not going to go away. I had tried to change it for years with prayer, distraction, and therapy. The fog-shrouded highway had finally closed in around me, and I was crashing, but now there were four of us in the car. And it was a bloody and tragic accident scene.

The lyrics to the chorus of a church song that I used to sing on Sundays went:

> *Here I am, Lord. Is it I, Lord?*
> *I have heard you calling in the night.*
> *I will go, Lord, if you lead me.*
> *I will hold your people in my heart.*

Over the years as I desperately tried to hold on to my marriage and family, I shed many tears in church and at home as I prayed these words, "Here I am, Lord. Is it I, Lord? I have heard you calling in the night. I will go, Lord, if you lead me. I will hold your people in my heart."

PART II

A LIFE FOUND

8

THE DETOUR

AFTER I LEFT MY POSITION at the fire department, I began my master's degree. When I graduated, I was hired as a research associate at the university. At this time, I was still hanging on to my marriage and family; all that anguish and turmoil was yet to come. The work was supposed to be in my field of fire management and fire ecology, but the funding never panned out. In the meantime, a professor hired me to collect field data and conduct laboratory analysis on water samples. If when I die, I end up in hell, this is how I might spend my eternity. But I needed an income, so it fit the bill.

One day, after a few months of mind-numbing science, a fire agency out west offered me a full-time position for the summer. I would lead five fire engines, a twenty-person hand crew, and a water tender. I would supervise thirty-five firefighters for the summer and would be moved around the state fighting fires where needed. It took me about fifteen seconds to say yes. I escaped the lab and went west for adventure and money.

But I was still married and hadn't asked my wife's opinion, though the kids were in high school and junior high and didn't need my constant supervision. Plus, I honestly thought the more time I spent away from home, the longer my marriage might last. If I wasn't around, I reasoned, my wife was less likely to tell me she wanted a divorce. I would be back in the West, surrounded by the mountains and wildlands that

I loved so much, and I would be working long hours, making a lot of overtime. It seemed like a smart move, and it would provide me with opportunities that would save my future career.

When I came back at the end of that summer, I decided to try my hand at another adventure. All my life I had been an avid gardener. I'd spent my formative years hiking through my desert home, identifying and familiarizing myself with the vegetation around me. I loved growing flowers. I loved flower arranging. I loved all things botanical, and still do. I saved my money from fire work that summer, and with my wife's hesitant agreement, I bought a flower shop.

It was a major divergence from my career path, but it seemed like it could be fun. I knew nothing about running a flower shop, but I had an eye for design and was confident that I could be successful. As a good friend used to say about herself, "I may not always be right, but I'm always confident."

Customers rightly expect a certain level of professional skill from a successful floral designer. You need more than imaginative ideas: you need the technical expertise to know how to build designs with different flowers. I signed up for several floral design classes to make sure I had the technical skills to back up the design eye that I thought I had. Indeed, my work was pretty good, and the teacher—who owned multiple flower shops throughout the Southwest and Southern California—invited to me to more advanced classes that he hosted in Los Angeles.

While at one of the classes in California, I was dressed like I normally was: jeans and a T-shirt or sweatshirt. I had made the decision long ago to give up my constant performance of gender, and people weren't exactly sure if I was a man or a woman. If I needed to be perceived as masculine, I tried to talk a certain way and stand a certain way. But this took effort. If I didn't "act," people tended to think I was a woman.

During the workshop we teamed up to work in pairs. One of the other students in the class was an attractive woman about my age. We struck up an instant friendship and worked together on all our projects, laughing and having a good time. She was an accomplished floral designer and had many more years of experience than I had, but I had enough talent and ability to keep up.

One morning, one of the teachers came up to me and said, "So, I need to know if you're Bobby with a *y* or Bobbie with an *ie*. It's no big deal, but are you transitioning?"

I didn't know what to say exactly.

"Does it matter?" I replied. "I guess call me Bobbie if that makes it easier."

It didn't matter to me. I wasn't changing my look for the class, but I felt like it gave me permission to put on some lipstick in the morning. The lipstick was enough to erase any confusion from those around me. It was done. At least for a week or so while in California, I would be Bobbie.

There were several guys who were around the class, bringing in buckets of flowers and supplies we needed, helping to clean up after the students made some huge banquet floral bouquets. They were nice and polite, and I realized that they took every opportunity to come and hang out at our worktable to talk with us. I assumed they were there to put the moves on my work partner. She was an attractive redhead with a good figure. They couldn't have been hanging around for me.

One afternoon, they said to the both of us, "Hey, why don't you girls come with us tonight? We're going to go out for drinks and hit some clubs. We'll have a good time."

I stared at them. "Hmm, I don't know," I mumbled.

My friend was giggling and smiling back, but I was very unsure. Our instructor had apparently heard the exchange and came over to our worktable and looked at the both of us.

"You had better be sure you want to go out with those two. It could be a wild evening, knowing them."

Holy smokes! I thought. *I am not ready for this.*

I realized I was too naive. We passed on their invitation.

The flower shop I had purchased back home was an established business in a town about forty miles away from where we lived. There were no flower shops for sale any closer to home, and I thought the distance would be better for my family and me. The previous owner was an elderly woman. The business had been booming back in her day, but now the interior of the shop was as old and tired as she was.

There were several employees that came with the store. They were wonderful women, and I became friends with all of them. They knew I was married and had even met my wife, but they gradually figured out my unique circumstance. When a customer asked to see me, rather than saying "I'll go get her" or I'll go get him," they would answer, "I'll go get Bobbie for you."

It must have been a peculiar situation for them, but they were wonderful about it all. I confided to them that I was trying to hold on to my marriage but struggled with my gender—which was obvious to anyone who got to know me.

Along with my regular employees who helped make arrangements, process flowers, and tend to the customers, there was also a group of elderly women who had been friends with the previous owner. I called them my "Baptist Church Ladies." The leader of the Baptist Church Ladies was my bookkeeper. She was in the shop a few times a week and paid my bills and prepared my taxes each month. Lorraine was a proper and kind church lady. She always wore a skirt, blouse, and jacket. Her blouses were the high-necked ruffled type. She was a wonderful woman who became my friend and confidant. Lorraine and the other Baptist Church Ladies were all friends from the big Baptist church around the corner from the flower shop.

These women had been coming into the shop to help with the holiday overflow business for years. Every Christmas, Valentine's Day, Easter, and Mother's Day, I could count on them to come in en masse to assist at the front counter or in the back making up orders. They were a godsend. I would have been less successful without them.

Eventually, my crumbling marriage came tumbling down. My wife had finally worn out. It didn't help that she could no longer ignore how people saw me. When my Church Ladies came in to work one of the busy holidays, one of them saw my red, puffy eyes and took me off to the side.

"What's the matter, Bobbie? I can tell you've been crying. Tell me what's the matter."

By this time, I had become a regular part of their comings and goings. Even though I was attending the Catholic church and participating in my own church's religious and social events, the Baptist Church

Ladies asked me to help ferry some of the older people who couldn't drive themselves to Christmas events at their church around the corner or to visit an elderly shut-in just to check on them. I had become a part of their circle, and to be honest, they were an important part of my life. These women had become surrogate moms to me. So when one of them wanted to know why I was crying, I began to sob even more.

"I'm getting divorced," I said. "My wife said she can't be with me anymore because I'm not masculine enough."

In truth, my wife had told me that even though I had been androgynous throughout our life together, now it wasn't OK. It wasn't enough for her anymore. Now I had to be totally masculine. It was then that I knew our marriage would certainly end. How was I supposed to start being masculine after forty years of struggling with the act? When my sweet church lady heard from me that I was getting divorced, she took my shoulders in her hands and looked closely into my eyes.

"Oh honey, look at you. You can't be a man. You're not like a man."

She hugged me tight, and I cried.

I was crying for my lost life. But I was also crying because this caring, loving older conservative Baptist Church Lady could see me. She could see me through the tatters of the old, frayed cloth that had covered me for so long. The covering was now gone. And the sweet older church lady reminded me so much of my own mother and the love and acceptance I'd missed getting from my own family growing up. It was sweet, it was scary, and it was heartbreaking.

I hired a high school student to come in every afternoon after school. Her job was to sweep up, help around the shop, and make whatever deliveries that still had to be made for the day. She reminded me of my daughter. When Father's Day rolled around, I received a package from my daughter, who was about the same age as my employee. In the package was a mixed cassette tape of songs that my daughter had recorded for me. I still have it.

When she saw my cassette tape, my young employee said, "How cool is that! Your daughter sent you a present for Father's Day."

With a quizzical look on my face I said, "What's so weird about that? I mean, I am her father."

The poor girl just stared at me. She backed up and leaned up against the wall behind her.

"Oh my gosh! I'm so sorry," I said. "I assumed you knew I was a guy."

It had never occurred to me that she didn't know. The girls never told her, apparently, and it had never come up. But it made little difference to her. We worked together often and laughed. We always had a good time working together.

My insurance agent for my business had his office just down the street from my flower shop. He had always been friendly to me and helped me get the best policy and price. Nearly once a month he'd walk down the street from his office to my shop to order flowers for his current girlfriend. Because he was tall, fit, and very good looking, whenever he came into the store all the girls working for me would try to push past each other with elbows flying to be the first one to the front sales counter to wait on him. It got to be such a fun drama. It made me laugh because the southern accents on the girls got thicker: "Why, hi, Tim,* how're you today?" said in a sweet-as-tea southern accent. Sometimes I would pull rank and say, "Stay here and work; I'll wait on him." They'd grumble and pout but would go back to their chores, and I'd go up front to wait on this nice gentleman. We took turns delivering his flowers. Everyone always wanted to see what his latest girlfriend looked like, so whoever delivered that month's flowers for Tim came back to the shop and described her. It was great sport.

Tim was in the US Army reserve. But even when he was in civilian clothes, he had that military look about him. Short, cropped hair, physically fit—and he carried himself with the self-assurance and confidence of the military officer he was.

By this time, my divorce had been finalized, and I had quit worrying about my gender. I had some lovely casual blouses, but I still just wore jeans. I never dressed up to be overtly feminine. It just wasn't me. I was still going on temporary fire assignments during the summer because the flower business was slow, and I could make decent money a few weeks at a time. Between Lorraine, my bookkeeper, and the girls who worked for me, the flower shop was handled just fine. So I was still the firefighter-florist.

---

* Pseudonym

One time, when Tim came into the shop, the girls started fighting for the pole position to wait on him. But I gave them all the dirty eye and pulled rank on them. They reluctantly backed off.

I went up to wait on Tim, and he said, "No flowers today. Want to talk, Bobbie?"

I was surprised. I was worried that there was a problem with my insurance policy. Maybe the rates were going up. Oh no. I couldn't afford one more bill to increase.

"Sure," I said. "Come sit down over here."

I led him to a little area I had set up for brides and their moms to look over floral arrangement ideas for their weddings. It was out of the way and out of earshot of my good friends and employees.

"What's the matter, Tim?" I was worried. His eyebrows raised up.

"What's the matter? Nothing's the matter, why do you ask?"

"Well, you're not ordering flowers, for starters," I said. "Is something wrong with my insurance?"

"No, no, no," he smiled and chuckled. "I just wanted to talk."

I was confused. "You just want to talk? OK, sure, we can talk." Even though my wife and I had been separated for nearly a year, I had only been divorced for a few weeks and was still emotionally weak.

We sat on my lovely little antique love seat and talked. It was a relaxed conversation between friends, which we had become over the couple years of doing business together.

Finally, he said, "Can I come over tonight? Do you want to go somewhere for drinks? How about dinner or a movie?"

I went from being relaxed and enjoying the conversation to feeling anxious and afraid. I couldn't date anyone. I was just barely divorced—plus I was still technically a male. "Oh, Tim, don't you know my story?" I asked.

"Sure," he replied. "I know you used to be a guy. But you have to know after all the conversations we've had, I find you very attractive. Surely you know that."

Inside my head I thought, *What? What? You find me attractive?* I felt that I lied by omission that day. I didn't tell him that I had not had surgery yet. Oh my gosh, I was freaked out.

I told him that I couldn't go on a date with him, but I could meet him after church on Sunday morning for coffee. For a few weeks on Sundays after church, I'd meet Tim for coffee. It was my first sort-of date. Eventually, when Tim wasn't making any headway with me, we stopped meeting for coffee. I was disappointed but grateful for those times of talking and enjoying his company. It gave me confidence and a glimpse that maybe men might find me attractive.

Shortly after my coffees with Tim, I went by myself on a ski trip. Skiing had always been an important activity for me. Over the years when it was available, I skied once a week. But skiing wasn't close to me while I owned the flower shop, so I made the effort to go alone and drove to New Mexico for a lonely ski trip. Since skiing had always been my family activity, I was painfully forlorn to go on my own, but I missed the beautiful mountains and needed to feel the cold air on my face.

I was only there for a couple days when one night at dinner, a gentleman sitting alone at a nearby table struck up a conversation. He was polite and didn't seem pushy.

We ended up joining each other for dinner and had a nice evening. We met up the next day after skiing for dinner once again as well. I recognized that he was becoming interested in me, but I couldn't let anything develop. I was new to dating. I was new to being seen totally as a woman, and I was too anxious to let a relationship develop.

Before I left to drive eastward through a Texas blizzard and go home, he started making plans to come visit me. I said no. I didn't explain why, just no. He would call a few times a week once I was back to my flower shop. He wanted to come visit and take me for a ride on his motorcycle. It sounded scary—but exhilarating.

I decided to tell him my story. I assumed that once he knew, he would not want to come visit me. But to my surprise, he said, "That's OK, we'll figure it out." I don't know how much he really understood, but he was going to ride his motorcycle cross-country to visit me.

The girls at the shop followed my social adventures like a television series. They knew about Tim, and now they knew about Phil.* When

---

* Pseudonym

Lorraine came in one afternoon to work on the books, the girls said, "Lorraine, did you hear Phil is coming to visit Bobbie?"

She looked up at me over her reading glasses and took them off, letting them hang from the decorative chain around her neck.

"Phil is coming to visit you?"

"Um, yes, he is," I replied. I didn't know if she would say she'll pray for my lost soul or if she was just going to get up and leave. I mean, how much can you push a sweet but conservative Baptist church lady? She asked when he was coming, and I told her the weekend a month away.

"We're going on a cruise that week," she said. "Phil can stay at our home. As a matter of fact, I'll make up the guest room, and you can both use the house for the weekend. I mean, there's no sense in Phil renting a hotel room with our home sitting empty."

"Um . . . what? Phil can stay at your home while you're gone?" I asked for clarification. I knew I must have misheard.

"You can both stay at our house while he's here."

My head was spinning. My plan was for Phil to stay at a hotel while he visited. I wasn't going to invite him to stay with me for two reasons. First, my little apartment was tiny and built into the shop. There was hardly any room for even me. Second, I was too freaked out about the idea of being next to, let alone sleeping with, a man. But here was one of my surrogate moms telling me that a guy that I had recently met could stay at her home while they were off on a cruise—and I could stay with him. It was a head-scratcher.

Nervously, I responded, "Thanks, that's very nice of you to offer," in a tiny voice.

When Phil came, he gave all the girls at the shop a ride on his big motorcycle, and they loved it. I loved it too. And when we stayed at Lorraine's home, my nervousness and morals kept anything from happening. But we slept in the same bed, and that was a first for me.

Phil and I kept in touch and saw each other a few more times. But I was in no way ready for a relationship. I had too much to do before anything like that could happen. And for all I knew, Phil was just having a fling.

9

THE DANCE

AFTER MY DIVORCE, I FELT like I had been set adrift. I remember thinking about herd animals and how, when one of them is sick, they get left behind by the herd.

I felt like I had lost my herd.

My mom and dad were coming from their religious Italian beliefs and fears, telling me that if I didn't repent, I'd be going to hell. I wasn't sure what I was supposed to repent about. I had not invented my gender issues. My wife had kicked me out of the house and divorced me. My brothers thought I had torn my family apart for selfish reasons and that I was just confused about who I was. One of my brothers allowed me to live in his home for a couple months while I was getting back on my feet. It was really his wife that insisted that I come stay with them: I lived in their home, but he was never nice to me. It was very uncomfortable, but to his credit he didn't say no, and for that I will always be grateful.

I did have some family who remained my faithful friends. A few cousins and two aunts. Both of my aunts were also from the "old country" and were loving and kind to me. They, too, became like surrogate moms. When my aunt learned about my recent divorce and the breakup of my family, she told my cousin, "There isn't another woman; it's because Bobbie is a woman."

My cousin had never seen it herself. But my elderly aunt from Italy had seen through my disguise for years and understood. It's funny how some people knew—maybe always knew—while others didn't.

I purposely distanced myself from many of my friends. I was embarrassed. And I was still living in limbo between being a man and being a woman. I think many people feel uncomfortable when they can't put a person into one of two genders. We have a need to categorize people. When a person can't easily be categorized, it makes those around them uncomfortable. I don't know that to be scientifically accurate, but it's what I've observed. The only thing I'm an expert on is me.

Six months after my divorce was final, I was still going to therapy. I had to talk to someone. My world had collapsed, and I was still struggling with what my future might look like. Should I even have a future? In my mind, taking action to short-circuit and end my life was still on the table. I desperately missed my children. I missed my ex, but it was my kids that I longed for. But they were gone. It seemed so final. Even if I prayed and hoped to be back in their lives, it wasn't going to happen.

Once I was divorced, I stopped worrying about trying to pass as a man. I stopped making any effort to look "masculine." I didn't care anymore. Who was I trying to be a man for now? I began taking time with my hair, makeup, and nails. For the first time in my life, I was able to look in the mirror and see me. I saw what others had seen for years. In my warped perceptions while growing up, I thought I would never be able to look like an ordinary woman. Even while I was being mistaken for one, I still thought I was too masculine-looking. But now, I could finally see me.

People I've known over the years have tried to compare being gay to being transgender. I would ask them while they were making the comparison if they thought that in the morning when a gay man or woman looks in the bathroom mirror, that person really sees themselves. Do they see the person they are, or do they see someone else?

The answer was always the same.

"Of course they see themselves."

"When I look in a mirror," I would say, "I don't see me. I see a man looking back. That's not me. I can't see me at all."

But now when I looked in the mirror, I could finally see me. Not the me I had always wanted to be. I saw *me*. The me I always was.

It was as if a giant weight had been lifted off my chest. I could breathe.

By now, I was going out for a beer with my girlfriends or playing volleyball or cards with my friends from the church "single, divorced, and widowed" group. As miserable as I was being separated from family, I felt some sense of relief being around a new set of friends with shared values. No one ever knew about my gender issues. They all assumed I was just another divorced woman. I had a new social life. We were all injured souls, so I fit right in.

Throughout my life, men had often made sexual advances toward me. I always shunned those moves because I never felt like a gay man. I thought I was always presenting as a straight man and wasn't interested in being in a gay relationship. After I left the fire department and grew my hair out, men would ask me to dance if I was out with friends listening to music. Or a man I knew socially might ask me out for a drink. I steered clear of any such complications. I was still married back then. And while I might have been trying to find a balance between male and female, if I assumed people thought I was male and a man made an advance toward me, I had absolutely no interest in responding positively toward him. Not until guys were responding to me as a typical middle-aged female did I finally feel romantic affirmation.

But now, after my divorce, even though I had not had my gender affirmation surgery, I was presenting myself as the woman I was. I still dressed like I always had with slacks and sweaters, but now I allowed myself to wear more feminine tops. I fixed my hair and wore makeup. Now the guys I was around began to ask me to dance when we were out with a group or asked me out on a date.

I cautiously started to date. Any date I went on during this period of my life presented a very real risk. I still had male genitalia. But for the first time in my life, I felt comfortable around men. I enjoyed their company, and they made me feel pretty and desired. It felt normal and natural.

Up until this point, I thought men were something I had to tolerate. I didn't really like them, although I had affection for those coworkers of mine who had become friends. For the most part, though, I thought men were Neanderthals. It became clear to me why I had felt this way. These cisgender, heterosexual men treated other men completely differently from how they treated women. When men treated me like any other guy, I found their behavior brutish and uncouth. I didn't like them. But slowly over time, men began treating me like they treated other women.

It was nothing like how I had been treated by men earlier in my life. Guys began holding doors open for me, their gaze lingering a tad longer than normal. It made me blush, but it felt so nice to be noticed. But most of all, men would just talk to me differently. It would present problems for me in the future as a female fire chief, but for now, it was amazing.

I'll never forget my first dance with a man. I was out listening to a band at a small club with one of my best friends. It was nothing fancy, and I wore my normal attire of jeans and a sweater. I was *not* on the prowl. Two guys asked if they could sit down with my friend and me to buy us a beer. They were typical small-town guys. Jeans and boots, nice-looking rural kind of guys. My friend had known me for years, so she knew my gender history, knew about my ex, knew all about my emotional turmoil. But on this night, she thought I needed to step out and have some "personal growth." We sat and talked for a while when one of the guys asked me to dance. I cautiously said yes and walked to the dance floor with him. The band had been playing a mix of rock and blues, so when the music started, we began a typical fast dance. I always loved to dance to good live music, so I just let myself enjoy the experience.

When the music was over, I was nervous and relieved to go back and sit at the table. I think my friend must have primed the other guy sitting at our table because as soon as I sat down, he immediately asked me to dance. I tried to demure. "No thank you, I don't want to dance any more tonight."

"Bobbie is just shy; she really wants to dance with you," my friend said with a grin.

Oh my gosh, I wanted to kill her! This was all moving too fast. In a friendly, teasing way, the gentleman was not going to take no for an answer. He thought I was acting shy, and my friend was egging him on. At one point I remember putting my head on the table and pulling my sweater over myself trying to hide. In retrospect, I think this was just more enticing to him. I finally relented and agreed to dance the next song with him. Before the next song started, he grabbed my hand as we walked up to the dance floor and waited for the song to begin. The music started. It was a slow song. Oh, my God, I can't dance a slow dance! I was freaked out. How could I dance a slow dance with a man?

"I'm sorry, I can't slow dance with you," I told him. "I just got divorced!"

He laughed and said, "I'm not asking you to marry me; it's just a dance."

I realized I was looking silly and allowed him to put his arms around me as we swayed to the music. He was tall and strong and nice and had a great smile. And I felt like I'd found home after forty years of my life.

It wasn't his arms that were home, but they represented a relationship with men that I had been hiding from my whole life. It was a completely new and wonderful feeling. Being held and led on the dance floor, I laid my head against his chest. It was life changing. Suddenly, I realized that I liked men. I mean I *really* liked men. I found home in the arms of a man I didn't even know. When the dance ended, I sat back down at our table, looked at my friend, and said, "We have to leave now."

Maybe it was just a dance, but I had to collect my thoughts. My friend obliged, but she was delighted because she knew something about me that I hadn't even considered or dreamed of for myself.

The next morning I called my therapist. I told her I needed an appointment right away. I drove the twenty-five minutes to the next town where her practice was and told her about my experience the night before and how it made me feel. Up until that point, I thought after the divorce I would simply stay single. I even considered joining a religious community. Even though I had been married to a woman for twenty years, I knew I wouldn't do that again. And since I wasn't gay, I wouldn't be with a man, so where did that leave me?

Speaking with my therapist allowed me to focus on my future. I needed to start thinking longer term. I needed a job. I had to start paying child support. I would need insurance and a reliable car. The only profession I really knew—and had multiple degrees in and loved—was firefighting.

It was after that slow dance that I decided to get moving with my life. As terrible a thought as it was to me at the time, I decided I was going to have to move back to the western United States and go back to work as a firefighter. It was a terrible thought because I would be moving further away from my children. But as things were, I wasn't allowed to see them, and I had no money to pay child support and no hope of being in their lives.

How was I going to live my life? If I was going to be a woman, I had to finally deal with the big issue I had been thinking about for nearly forty years. When I was a child, I laid in my bed saying a child's prayer for God to "fix" me. I knew what that meant. I wanted my little penis gone. Girls didn't have penises. I knew it all the way back then, and here I was all these years later realizing this was it. I had come as far as I could in this body. It was time to change course and find some clear road.

In 1998 I decided that in order to live an ordinary life, I was going to have to have surgery and finally be a woman on the outside as well as the inside. Without surgery I wouldn't be able to work as a firefighter again and live life as my true self. Firefighters have male and female shower facilities and bathrooms. I wouldn't be able to have an ordinary existence if I continued in this gender-hybrid reality that I had been living in. My lifelong dream was to be and feel "normal." That was it. I wasn't looking for fame and fortune, beauty, or any other traditional common wishes. I just wanted to be normal. After a lifetime of feeling anything but, I decided my only option to feel normal was to have gender reassignment surgery (or GRS).

One summer day, I drove to my therapy appointment. Speaking to my therapist was always very comforting for me. I trusted her judgment. It wasn't just because she was smart and had a PhD. She also belonged to my church, and we shared similar moral values. Over the years, my ex-wife had attended some of the counseling sessions with me. Those interactions helped my therapist understand all the dynamics of our family. Many of my sessions in her office were filled with tears and fear of the future. But she had no hidden agenda, and I had no anxiety over her judging my behavior. Her sole intent was to help me live a happy well-adjusted life.

Once I made my decision, I told her. "My kids will not see me. My entire family has shunned me," I said. "I don't know why I'm still trying to hang on to being a male. I think I'm ready to have GRS and get on with my life."

She just looked at me.

"I've been waiting to hear you say that," she replied.

I wept. It was the final acknowledgment. I finally admitted to myself that after a lifetime of wishing, praying, and hoping that I could be a normal woman, I would be taking the ultimate action to make it happen.

The process to have gender reassignment surgery is not simple. In 1998 there was a specific process that one had to go through for a surgeon to approve a patient for the surgery. Even today, there is a wide dichotomy between those who believe that there should be no rules and requirements to have GRS and those (like me) who believe that, for the sake of the patient, there should be extensive psychological evaluations to make sure that the patient isn't having other issues manifesting as gender dysphoria. I'm not suggesting that roadblocks be put up by medical professionals, but rather that the medical profession should practice due diligence to make sure that an emotionally fragile person doesn't undergo GRS for the wrong reasons.

At the time, the medical standards required me to have letters from two different certified therapists stating that I was emotionally healthy and was indeed a good candidate for GRS. Another requirement was the candidate for GRS had to have lived as the gender that they were transitioning to for at least a year in order to prove they were able to work and live successfully in their "new" gender.

Fortunately, I already had a therapist to provide one letter to the surgeon. My therapist recommended another therapist in a city four hours from me for my second letter. The other therapist specialized in gender issues and had a large list of patients that he treated. I called to make an appointment and attended the very next group session for his patients. Up to this point, I had only met one other transgender person. And that person was an Episcopal priest, so her values and mine aligned.

I nervously made the four-hour drive through the countryside for my first group session where I would meet many other transgender people. I was nervous and anxious, but excited, because now that I had made the decision to have surgery, I could imagine a future when, just a few months earlier, I hadn't been able to picture what mine might look like.

The therapist's office was an old home in a historical part of the city. It had been converted into offices and a large meeting room. I took a deep breath and walked into the office, found the other patients gathering in the large meeting room, and looked around for the doctor. He knew I was coming and immediately made me feel welcomed. I was still very nervous.

When we were all seated in a big circle, I looked at my fellow patients. In this big room with its tall ceilings and old wood floors, I started to get more anxious. The doctor introduced me to the group and asked me to say a few things so the others could get to know me. To my uneducated and parochial self, the other patients looked like they had issues other than being transgender. They spoke of homelessness and drugs. They looked at me like I was some soccer mom who had showed up to the wrong meeting at the community center. Normally, I would be making silent jokes in my head about it. But I became more concerned. Are these my peers? Is this who I am too? I had a job. I had a place to live. I owned a car.

I didn't say much.

I've been a fairly traditional person throughout my life. It may not seem so, but from where I sit, my life has been one of "mainstream" or expected living. Other than being trans—which I recognize is out of the ordinary—my life was almost mundane. I went to school, graduated, got married, had two kids, and had a career.

Though I was experiencing extreme turmoil as I reeled from my marriage ending and making the decision to officially transition, I was still a churchgoing business owner who belonged to the local chamber of commerce. I wasn't living on the edge. The fact that I blended into society was nothing I could take credit for—in fact, I was thankful that I looked feminine enough to look ordinary. I didn't stand out. And that made my life less complicated than some other transgender people.

When I met the trans people attending my first group session, I was uncomfortable because they didn't look like me. My social circle at the time were the other members of my divorced, widowed, and singles church group. We all looked like typical suburban, middle-class forty-somethings. But those attending this group session looked different. Their lives had been much more difficult than mine; the wear and tear was evident on their faces.

I never thought of myself as having had an easy life, but my life had definitely been easier than those sitting in the circle with me. My discomfort might have been in part because those folks sitting around me looked uncomfortable. But my discomfort could have simply been because I worried that I was one of them.

I *was* one of them, but I couldn't identify with them either.

After the group session was over, the doctor called me into his office and told me to sit down. He told me to write him an e-mail about who I was. Why did I want to have surgery? He told me to make it comprehensive so he could get an understanding of who I was. After a few hours of the group session and talking with the doctor, I was back on the road driving home, wondering what I should put in the letter to him. I would see him in a month at the next group session, and we would talk more then.

The next time I saw my regular therapist, I told her of my experience at the group session. I told her just how uncomfortable I felt while I was there. Was my discomfort because I could see myself in them? Did they look and behave differently because they had been shunned for so long that some ended up on the streets? Did they have other emotional challenges?

Instead of offering some level of understanding or agreement, she said I was a snob.

I felt insulted. I just couldn't see that I had very much in common with some of the people in the group session. I had lived a very traditional, sheltered lifestyle in small towns and suburbs. I had been going to work, school, raising kids, going to church, and singing in the church choir. My gender issues were easy in some respects. I could be myself with no concerns because I looked like an ordinary woman. I had never been exposed to alternatives to my small-town traditional life. But in this group, I met people who were very different from me, and that difference made me uncomfortable—just like others might be uncomfortable around me.

But in order to get my second letter from a mental health professional, I had to go back and sit in the circle. I knew I would have to participate more the next time. I just shrugged my shoulders and figured it was just another mountain to climb. Heck, it wasn't even a mountain. This was just a little hill.

The next month, I made the trip back to the group session. I walked into the old, remodeled house and sat in one of the chairs in the circle and waited for the session to begin. It was just like the month before. Some of the people there had some serious emotional problems. Some of those problems were medical, some of them involved work, and some were indeed gender related. I'm sure if I had gotten to know some of the others there, I would have realized that many were just like me.

When the therapist came in, he started the discussion and made sure I talked more about me this time. I had to explain my hope to have surgery and why. I described my plans for the next few years. How I wanted to go back to being a firefighter and just live an ordinary life. I sensed that they thought that maybe I was the odd one.

After the session was over, the therapist called me into his office. He told me to sit down. When I did, he gave me an envelope with his letter inside. It was my second letter to give the surgeon. I was shocked!

"You already wrote the letter," I said.

"Yes," he replied.

"Wait, you should be asking me all sorts of questions. You should be making sure I'm really a transsexual and not just mixed up," I said. I continued for a few minutes, telling him what his job was and how I was concerned that he wasn't practicing due diligence.

He said, "I read your long e-mail. I've spoken to you several times now both on the phone and twice in person. Let me ask you, are you like the folks in the next room?" He was motioning to the large meeting room where most of the group were still present and talking.

It almost felt like a trick question. After being called a snob by the therapist I had known for years, I was cautious answering this new therapist. Am I like those people in the next room?

"Well, not to be rude, but no," I said. "I don't have all those problems. I have many of my own problems, but I am not like them."

I thought he might call me a snob too. Instead, he said, "You have your letter. Now go and make a good life for yourself."

That was it. I had my two letters now.

The third requirement was to live as a woman for a year before surgery. The purpose of this requirement was to demonstrate the patient's ability to work and live as the gender they identified as before the irreversible surgery. My situation might have been a bit unique. I had been living in gender limbo for long enough. My regular therapist already knew I would be able to live and work as a woman.

There were several good and reputable gender surgeons in the United States. The going price to have GRS in the United States at the time was about $20,000. I had little money after my divorce. I had a small retirement account from when I worked for the university after receiving my master's degree, but it didn't even have half of the $20,000 I would need. I didn't have medical insurance either, but in 1998, I don't think any insurance companies covered GRS in the United States.

I did as much research as I could to find a surgeon. One of the surgeons who had a great reputation and had done thousands of surgeries was in Canada. And in the late '90s, the exchange rate between the United States and Canada was definitely in my favor. If I went to Montreal, I could have my surgery, and it would cost me $7,600 plus my airfare. God bless the exchange rate. Without it, I don't know if I could have had my surgery.

I had been on the waiting list for an open surgery date for several months. The next firm opening was six months away. I was currently working as a consultant to a fire department, but I needed a job with benefits. I was behind on my child support and getting stressed. If I was going to go back to work for a federal wildland fire agency, I needed to have my surgery soon.

That December, I received a phone call from Montreal. A cancellation occurred, and there was an opening for my GRS in ten days. They needed an answer as quickly as possible. I called the doctor's office the next day and confirmed my surgery date.

Years later, after reconnecting with old friends, they asked me why I didn't invite a friend to come with me to Canada for the surgery as moral support. The truth was, I didn't want anyone to come. I didn't feel like I needed anyone. Having gender surgery is such a private issue. It seemed to me that I had to do this all on my own. I needed to be present in the moment as I prepared for and traveled to Montreal. There could be no more distractions to keep me from thinking about my life.

The repercussions of having gender affirmation surgery would be permanent and massive for me and my entire family. But I had already been expelled from the family. I was told not to attend the big family Christmas celebration with all the extended family. I was not invited to my daughter's high school graduation. There was no coming back from my surgery. Did I have any last nagging doubts in the back of my mind about my decision? No doubts. Surgery or no surgery, I was out of the family. I wanted to live now. I wanted to work and make friends and make a home and have a life. I just wanted to feel normal. And surgery would make my body congruent with my mind. Finally, after forty-four years, at least my mind and body would be in alignment.

I arrived in Montreal late on a Friday evening. The doctor's office had arranged for a limo to meet me at the airport. As I walked through the terminal with my bag, I spotted the row of limo drivers holding up signs with people's names on little white boards. There was my name, held by a gentleman in a black suit. I was a bit nervous, but so far, so good.

The limo driver drove me to a large residence that might have been built as a bed-and-breakfast. It was a two-story stone home in a rural but affluent area outside of Montreal. When we arrived, the driver took my bag to the door and walked in. It was nearly 10:00 PM when I arrived at the residence, and I was asked if I wanted something to eat. The cook always had food available. I said no thanks, and was shown to my room upstairs—one of nine bedrooms.

I felt like I had just landed on Mars. Everything was alien to me. It was my first time out of the country other than short trips to Mexico. But I still felt sure and confident in my decision.

The following morning, I met some of the other patients. Some of them were recovering from surgeries, and others, like me, were preparing for surgery. Not all the patients were transgender, as there were patients having other cosmetic surgeries. But there were two trans men. It was the first time I had ever been around a transgender man. One was a tall, dark, and handsome man with a short beard. He was a medical doctor back home in the United States. I was so happy to meet a successful transgender man living the kind of "mainstream" life I wanted so badly for myself. The other was in his twenties—and he behaved like every young guy I had ever met. In my mind, there was no doubt about his gender identity. For all intents and purposes from the outside, he looked like a young macho guy who was probably too full of himself. And I think he liked being surrounded by a house full of women.

My surgery was scheduled for Monday morning. But it was Saturday. I could only sit around and talk to the other patients so much. It was snowing and cold outside. The sidewalks were starting to gather about three or four inches of snow. I put on my jacket and went out to start shoveling snow. I was told, "No, no, you shouldn't be shoveling the snow!" But it was good for me. It was exercise, and I needed to use up some nervous energy.

On Sunday morning, I walked through the snow to the little town about two miles away and attended mass. It was entirely in French, but I said my prayers for the doctor, my children, my ex, and for me the next day. That night, the limo driver took me to the small hospital where I would have my surgery. I went to sleep that night saying my rosary.

Monday morning I went through all the regular presurgery checks and processes. They asked me if I wanted to walk or be wheeled into the surgical suite. I chose to walk. It seemed fitting that I should walk on my own down the hall. Traveling to Canada on my own and then walking myself down the hallway to the surgical suite were very important to me.

All my life, I had ended up doing things by default. I tried to play high school football because my family said I should. I became a firefighter because it was something I could do to prove myself. I got married because it was expected and I was told it was time. For some reason, I recognized that going to Montreal by myself and then walking down the hall in the hospital on my own power—not being pushed in a wheelchair or gurney—was me demonstrating that this was my choice. It was me. On my own and without anyone's direction or influence, I was going to resolve a major issue in my life.

10

THE SEARCH
FOR CALM WATER

AFTER RECOVERING FROM GENDER AFFIRMATION surgery, I moved back to the West, back to my familiar and comforting mountains and deserts. That cross-country trip in my pickup truck was a wretched and pitiful journey. I tried to revisit some of my favorite places in Arizona and Colorado, yet I was overwhelmed with guilt of having left my babies, immersed in the pain. The shame and feeling of defeat enveloped me. There was no enjoyment in seeing my mountains, no reprieve to be had. But I was traveling, and traveling means change: a change of scenery, a change of topography, a change of self, and another change—the surgery that made my transition feel complete and official. I could change my birth certificate. I could take showers at work using the women's bathrooms. So much of the daily anxiety of guessing how other people saw me was alleviated, and I could live my life more fully. Without seeing how or when, I knew I was on a trail toward a healthier me. I just didn't know how to deal with not being in my children's lives. That loss haunts me to this day.

Before I left the Midwest and my family, I printed up dozens of copies of my resume to distribute across the country like playbills on Broadway. I stopped at many national forest offices along the way and inquired about fire jobs. I had given up on going back to a fire department. I was still too concerned about the culture and whether I could

survive it again. Instead, I was going to try and concentrate on the wildland fire agencies. With my master's degree and undergraduate studies,
I figured I should be a good candidate. But I would take the first job I
was offered. This was no time to be picky.

A couple years before, while on a wildfire in eastern Oregon, I
worked for a man whose name was Steve. He had been a bit of a hard-
ass. But surprisingly, when I was going through the demobilization
process and leaving the fire, he said to me, "You're the best division
supervisor I've ever had work for me. If you're ever looking for a job,
look me up."

While working for him, I was still male—albeit a male with a neutral
gender appearance. Now I was legally, physically, and visibly female.
Asking a rural blue-collar guy to accept the new me seemed like a lot
to ask. But I had to start somewhere. I thought I should contact him
and see if he had any openings. Even though I had nearly twenty-five
years of experience and multiple degrees, all I wanted was a low-level
job to get my foot in the door and a place to heal my battered soul.

Steve was welcoming and affirming. If he thought it was weird that
I was now a woman, he never said a thing. He gave me faith that I
could return to the work I loved. He didn't have a job for me, but
he made multiple calls to neighboring national forests and various fire
departments. I was thankful for his help, which gave me the confidence
I needed to be able to live my life as my realized, true self. Just live my
life. His assistance set me up for the rest of my career.

With Steve's help, the first job offer I received was from a friend
of his: a fire chief of a small department. It wasn't a full-time position,
but the department needed some higher-level planning work done. I
was hired as a consultant. The project really wasn't that complex, and
it shouldn't have taken very long, but the fire chief kept adding things
on to my work to keep me around. I was sure he was just being kind.
He kept telling me to stick around because "a permanent position
might just open up." I knew he was trying to find me something, but
after six months I had finished the project and was offered a permanent position with a federal wildland fire agency in California. I left
the safety of that little department and the friendship of the fire chief

and headed to the bright lights of California, not knowing that my life and career would intersect with Steve and the fire chief again in a few years.

My tenure in California was a mixed bag. The office I worked for seemed to have some odd personnel dynamics going on. Years after I left, I learned that the office manager had pled guilty to embezzlement of government funds. I think others in the office might have known there was some secret funny business afoot, which led to the discomfort I felt there.

Fighting wildfires in California can be amazing, and their uniqueness set me up for future successes too. These are big fires. Fires with a lot at risk. Homes and communities are in danger almost every time a new fire starts. When homes and lives are in peril, it raises the stakes for all the responders. Expectations are high and situations are dire; there's no choice but to perform at the top of your game. Contrast this with a fire starting in the backcountry in the wilderness, where nothing human might be at risk at all.

Unlike in many areas of the United States, most city fire departments in California are well trained in wildland firefighting and respond to assist the wildland agencies quickly and effectively. The state of California provides wildland fire protection to its jurisdiction through Cal Fire, the state fire department. Then there are the multiple federal wildland fire agencies such as the US Forest Service, Bureau of Land Management (BLM), and others. I was working for a federal agency but worked hand in hand with Cal Fire. Immediately I was responding to fires throughout the West as well as in my own area. I had found a home, even if only for a few years.

When a new fire chief arrives at a fire department or, in this case, to a federal land management agency, the personnel in the office wonder: Who is this new person? Do they really "know their stuff?" What's their background? Who do we know that might know them? Understandably, they want to know who this new leader is.

In California back in the 1990s, a female fire chief was doubly suspect. There had been a consent decree agreed to, ensuring women would have some priority for hiring. This meant that being a female fire chief in California wasn't exactly a good thing for trying to build trust and confidence with your coworkers. In a somewhat comical way, I think I was wondering the same thing: Who was I? It would take some time for me to figure it out. But I thank God that I was confident in my knowledge of firefighting and of leadership.

No one ever asked me about my past. No one ever said, "Did you used to be a guy?" Somehow, I portrayed some level of confidence. When I look back on myself in 1999, having only recently legally and physically changed my gender, lost my family, moved to a new state, and started a new job, I'm amazed I had the confidence I did. When leading a group, regardless of the endeavor, you need confidence for your personnel to trust you. Their trust then allows an organization to pull together to accomplish whatever goals are required. I was fortunate to be in a position where the personnel were looking for a leader. I was fortunate to be that leader.

Professionally, I was off and running.

If I looked confident and capable at work, I was a bit of an emotional mess when not at work. I was still reeling from rejection by my family, especially my parents and siblings. I had never been alone like I was in California. And because of that, I joined a book club that we later named the International Literary Guild and Wine Club.

It was made up of four or five women who were about the same age. We didn't know each other or anyone else in town—one woman was from the United Kingdom (which gave us the "international" in our moniker). We started meeting weekly to talk about the books we were reading, and within weeks, our book club meetings included wine. A few months after that, the books became less important, and the conversations, friendships, and wine became more essential. Everyone in the group had similar recent experiences: divorces and breakups were a common theme, and we all bonded. Since the books became less central to the group, we included a few other women who met the same criteria. It was my new support group. And they became critically important to my emotional well-being. With this group, I was open about my recent past. I was accepted without question. I loved those women.

Once again, work provided a helpful distraction and kept me busy. I was fortunate to respond to many fires and gained positive experiences as well as the respect of my coworkers. In addition to being dispatched to fires in California, now as a regular federal firefighter, I was dispatched to fires around the country.

It was in the southern Sierra Nevada Mountain Range where I established my credibility with the California organization. Or at least, it started in the mountains. It ended up well east of them. I was assigned as a division supervisor on the fire line and was responsible for a portion of the fire and directly supervising firefighters. It was familiar and comfortable ground to be working in.

After a few weeks of active firefighting and conducting big burn-outs (intentionally set fires between the main fire and the fire line) in order to save homes in the path of the fire, I was feeling pretty good. My coworkers were primarily Cal Fire battalion chiefs. These guys were grizzled, older fire chiefs. They knew their stuff, and they were constantly telling me what I should be doing, despite being my equals on the fire. I didn't work for them, and by God, I didn't need them telling me what to do. They would never tell another man what he should be doing, but they felt quite confident telling this cute younger woman what she should do.

Many of the critical burn-outs happened on my division, and my supervisor, the operations section chief, was happy with my performance. One day, while preparing to start burning out before the fire got to a small, remote rural subdivision, one of my strike team leaders refused to conduct the burn-out. At six-foot-four he towered over me, and he was convinced that I didn't know what I was doing. He didn't know that during my career, I had burned tens of thousands of acres in similar fuel types. Finally, after unsuccessfully trying to explain to him that conditions were perfect to conduct the operation, I'd had enough. I couldn't take his condescending language or his threatening posture.

"I know you might not know enough to conduct this burn-out, and that's OK," I said. "I'm going to send you back to camp where you'll wait for another assignment while I get a crew in here who can do the job."

In the modern work environment, we teach our firefighters how to appropriately turn down an assignment if they feel it is unsafe. And we teach our leaders how to lead effectively in these situations. But neither of us was taking the high road that morning on my division, and I deliberately chose to insult and demean him to fight back against his failed intimidation tactics.

When I told him that I was sending his strike team back to camp, he started to lunge at me. He was so angry that I thought *Oh my gosh, he's going to beat me up*. His crew members had to grab him and pull him away from me while he literally spit out his curse words at me.

My mouth went totally dry. I could barely speak, but I stood my ground. As his crew members held him back, I was able to tell them, "Get him in the truck, and get back to camp now! Get him out of here!"

I avoided getting beaten up—but only barely. I could have handled that one better. But he was so far over the line, and he represented every Neanderthal macho guy I had ever dealt with in my career. I stopped putting up with it.

I called the planning section chief on the radio and said I would explain later, but I wanted the strike team leader demobilized for cause. I asked her to keep his strike team of engines and get them a new strike team leader.

Our burn-out that day was textbook successful. It went exactly like I had planned it. While the crews were holding the lines later that afternoon, the operations section chief came out to see how it went. He was happy. The ops chief described to me the plan for tomorrow. We had miles and miles of open fire line, and the plan was to conduct a burn-out using a two-lane state highway as our fire line. It was to be a nine-mile burn-out with homes and a campground along the way. It was going to be complicated. He explained that there would be five strike teams of engines (twenty-five fire engines) and ten twenty-person hand crews.

It would be a big operation.

"Wow, that's going to be awesome," I said. "Who's going to run it?"

He looked down at me and said, "You, if you want to."

"Yep, I want to."

He drove off, and I started planning the next day's operation. I was happy and proud that I was being recognized as a good division supervisor by the operations section chief. But I still had to go back to camp and deal with my strike team leader.

When I got back to the fire camp/incident command post, I went to find the planning section chief, who handles all the orders for incoming and demobilized firefighters and resources. I explained to her what had happened. By coincidence she was the strike team leader's supervisor back at their home unit. She was the forest fire chief, and he worked in her organization. She was very supportive of me but asked if I would have a word with the guy. He wanted to apologize.

I found him sitting down as he waited for a ride to take him on a two-hour drive back to his station. He looked much smaller and less threatening as he sat on a step with his elbows on his knees and his head in his hands. When I walked up to him, he looked up and softly said, "Sorry."

All I could answer was, "Yeah."

At that moment, I felt sorry for him. He looked like a little boy who had gotten in trouble. I asked him if he thought it was possible that someone might know more about certain aspects of firefighting than he did. He agreed that was possible. I went on to explain that over the course of my twenty-five-year career I had burned thousands of acres in that exact fuel type. I knew what I was doing.

We spoke for a while. Finally, he said, "Is there any way I can stay? My chief isn't going to let me go off Forest for the rest of the summer because of this." He knew that meant no more responding to the big fires away from his district and less overtime.

I quietly told him, "No, you've got to leave; this was a big deal."

"I understand," he said softly.

He never said he was yelling at me because I was a woman, but he didn't have to. Sure, under different circumstances he might have argued with a male division supervisor—but he wouldn't have been threatening. He might not have even argued. He didn't see a competent, experienced, and educated division supervisor. He just saw some woman. Looking back on it now, it makes me smile.

The next day, I had more than three hundred firefighters working for me as we began the critical burn-out that would contain a mega-fire in southern California. I had briefed my operations chief on how I would run the burn-out. He concurred. My neighboring Cal Fire division supervisors were a little out of sorts because I was the one in charge of this. All good firefighters want to be where the action is, and my big burn-out was where the action was going to be that day. Keeping in character, they tried to tell me what to do and how to run my operation.

I simply sat there and said, "Thanks, I've got a plan already."

"Well, if you need anything, let me know," one of them said.

That was my cue.

"Yes, I do need something. As my fire engines keep moving forward as our burn-out progresses, could you and your resources take up the rear and make sure nothing crosses the line behind us?"

It was a reasonable request from an adjoining force, but he didn't like it. "I'm not going to bring up the rear on your operation!" he replied. He didn't want to be in the rear of my operation; he wanted to be in charge of my operation.

By the time our burn-out operation was in full force, he set aside his pride and brought his forces up behind mine to help hold the line. He might have been old and crusty, but he was a good firefighter, and he knew how important it was to guard the rear of our line.

By the end of the day, we had completed most of the nine miles, and my stock value in the California fire world had gone way up.

By default, or by design, I never mentioned gender in my work environment. I think I wanted to remain neutral on the subject. I never complained that I was treated differently than the men because I was a woman. To be honest, I was treated better as a woman fire chief than I had been treated as a guy who was perceived as not being masculine enough. (Interestingly, I didn't notice a change in how the women treated me. I always got along well with women.) I realized that the male personalities I was working with do much better with a competent female firefighter than they do with a competent but maybe a little feminine male firefighter. My life as a firefighter was much improved.

Another time I was dispatched to a fire in Montana. I drove my very cool-looking emergency-yellow fire command rig from central California to western Montana. There had been some major lightning storms that summer, and fires were burning all over the West. As I drove through northern Nevada toward Montana, I saw smoke plumes from numerous fires burning across the landscape. I drove past dozens of fires before coming to the one I was dispatched to, where they were waiting for me.

There were so many fires that summer that many across the West had a fraction of the necessary firefighters assigned to them. There were some fires with hundreds of firefighters when thousands were needed, and many more fires that had a dozen or two—or none at all. When there are more fires than firefighters available to fight them, the fires are responded to in terms of priority. Those that pose less of a threat to a community or critical resource, such as a municipal watershed, are on the bottom of the list to receive valuable firefighting resources.

An incident management team was assigned to the fire I was responding to in Montana. The incident management team is responsible for the overall running of the fire. The team is like a hotshot crew in that they might come from anywhere in the country once assigned to a particular fire. The team is supervised by the incident commander and has approximately fifty people working in logistics, planning, finance, and operations.

There were a few fire engines and hand crews assigned to my fire, but not many. When resources are scarce, middle-management positions bear the brunt of critical shortages. Specifically, strike team leaders and task force leaders—those positions that supervise multiples of fire engines, hand crews, bulldozers, and so on—were in short supply. There were more people on the incident management team overseeing the fire than firefighters physically fighting the fire.

When I arrived, I was told that the big-picture strategy was to keep the fire out of the nearby rural communities.

"Don't spend too much time or energy fighting the fire up in the mountains," I was told.

We would be playing a waiting game.

I was to take actions to slow the fire down, but I wasn't to waste the few resources assigned to me on direct suppression actions up in the mountains. It was a bit unusual to be told to limit suppression actions, but it makes good sense when firefighting resources are limited.

I was assigned a division on the fire that was huge by normal standards. Divisions are geographical areas of the fire. If you drew an outline of the perimeter of the fire and segmented it, you'd create multiple smaller divisions for crews to manage and work on. This is how we determined which firefighters would be stationed in which area.

My division started on one side of a mountain, went up through a high alpine meadow, over the other side of the mountain, and back down into the lodgepole pine forests below. It was larger than any division I had ever overseen. It wasn't too complex, but I had no firefighters assigned to me. It was just me and my eight-mile-long division.

I spent the first day becoming familiar with the area. The actual fire was still a few miles up on the mountain, and it was slowly creeping downslope toward my division. I had no fire line in place and no firefighting resources to put a line in yet, so I created a plan to follow once some resources were assigned to me.

The next morning, the operations section chief from the team, the person in charge of all the firefighters, came to me and said that there were still no fire engines or hand crews available but the incident management team had hired five or six local loggers with bulldozers and logging equipment. He asked if I could make any progress with these local resources. I will always take whatever resource are available to me. I said yes, and went to find and brief my "firefighters."

It was a motley-looking group. Loggers come dressed for work pre-greased and pre-dusty. I mean, with all due respect, these folks get filthy in the course of a day. They're running bulldozers and tractors, excavators and skidders. It's dirty, labor-intensive work. The workday hadn't even started, yet they looked like they had been at it for a while. Not only was I a woman, but also I was clean, I had all my teeth, and I was from California. To them, I looked like some exotic creature.

My truck sat in a parking lot of fire apparatus and command trucks. It was yellow, while all the others were Forest Service green or fire department red. I had had a custom bumper made, painted, and installed to fit a winch. Due to the weight of the bumper, I had to have a lift kit installed on the truck. I wasn't into fancy trucks, but this was what I drove.

Like me, it stood out.

After I briefed the loggers, I singled out the one whose appearance was a step above the others and assigned him to be in charge. I sent them to trailer their equipment on their lowboy trailers to my division, where we would be working. A lowboy trailer is a trailer made to transport bulldozers and other heavy equipment. It is designed to sit low to the ground so the equipment can be driven on and off the trailer and keep the center of balance low, hence the name. It would take them a few hours to get their equipment moved from the base camp up to where we would be working. While they were getting into position, I drove around a bit more to make sure I was placing the fire line in the correct location.

The incident management team had assigned a firefighter from the nearby Forest Service ranger station to be my local guide. She knew the ground. She had grown up there and even knew all the local loggers assigned to my division. She carried with her a small handheld CB radio. We don't use CB radios on fires. We have radios with designated frequencies for each specific fire and division on that fire. But the loggers used CB radios to communicate with each other, and my local guide was listening in to their conversations. She started to laugh, but I didn't know what she was laughing at. I could tell she was trying to hide her laughter from me. Once or twice I asked what was going on, but she just said, "Oh nothing . . . just those guys."

It was getting obvious that something funny was being said on her CB.

"Just tell me what's going on," I said, growing aggravated.

"Just listen."

She turned up the volume on her little radio, and I could hear my knucklehead loggers talking about the work they were assigned to. Their conversation was full of static, so I couldn't make everything out, but I could hear them saying "*Baywatch.*"

I looked at her. "So, what's *Baywatch*?"

She was laughing out loud now. "You don't know what *Baywatch* is?"

"I only know about the TV show," I replied.

"Yeah," she said. "The TV show."

Now I was getting a bit impatient. What did the stupid TV show *Baywatch* have to do with these redneck loggers on my fire? In my frustration I finally said, "So what, what does *Baywatch* have to do with anything?"

She was really laughing now. "You're *Baywatch*. They're calling you *Baywatch*."

"Huh, what? I'm *Baywatch*? Why are they calling me *Baywatch*?"

"You're a woman from California, driving a truck that looks exactly like the trucks on *Baywatch*."

Oh brother! This was going to be a challenge. I wasn't sure how I should I handle this group.

An hour or so later, I caught up with my loggers at the pre-identified meet-up spot. They had not yet finished unloading their equipment and were milling about not getting much done. I found the guy whom I had put in charge and talked to him about my plan and made sure that the equipment assigned was appropriate for what I wanted to do. He seemed agreeable, so after a few minutes talking to him, I started to walk back toward my truck. By now the loggers were gathered around the front of my truck. A couple of them were on their backs lying on the ground under my front bumper. Some of them were kneeling in front of my truck looking, while the rest looked like they were fondling my custom-made, custom-painted bumper.

This was my moment to make an impression that I was not like a character from the TV show *Baywatch*.

I would have loved to tell them about the bumper and why I had it. How the bumper had been made by the guy who built all of Chuck Norris's truck bumpers (a fact that meant nothing to me but seemed to impress all my redneck buddies). How the paint job was done to complement the truck and bumper's design. But no, that's not how this was going to go.

Using my best angry fire chief voice and with a scowl on my face I said, "Dammit, you guys! Haven't you ever seen a bumper before? Get up and get back to work! Time's wasting!"

They looked up at me with shock on their faces. They scrambled up from the ground and ran back to their pieces of equipment. The rest of the day we put in fire line. They did good work; they were respectful, and not one of them ever called me *Baywatch* again.

The same local loggers were frustrated with the overall management of the fire. They didn't think the higher-level managers overseeing the suppression efforts were being aggressive enough trying to put out the fire. Resources were limited, and there wasn't much else we could do, but that explanation didn't satisfy my hardworking, well-intentioned loggers. By this time, I had been assigned a few hand crews and a strike team leader to provide more supervision on the division. The fire had continued backing down the mountain and was at the fire lines we had put in a few days before. We were all actively fighting the fire now.

I don't recall exactly what happened and why, but one day I got into a big argument with a local Forest Service official. The official was not assigned to the fire, but they were upset with some suppression action I was taking. They thought I was being too aggressive and doing some damage to the natural resources. Keep in mind that I had a bachelor of science in natural resource management and a master's in forestry in addition to my fire administration coursework and twenty-six years of firefighting experience. I wasn't doing any damage to any resource. But this official was upset with me and my folks.

I stepped in and lost my temper. I rarely lose my temper, but I was feeling the frustration of a long fire season and of trying to do too much with too little for too long on the fire. And now a biologist was going to give me lessons on how to protect the natural resources from fire. We were standing out on a dirt road in the middle of my division. My voice was raised, and I got into a shouting match with the guy. I had been standing there alone with him when almost immediately his eyes got big, and he walked quickly back to his truck to drive away. I didn't know what caused his change of heart. When I turned around, the loggers were walking down the road in my direction. They were all carrying steel rods and big wooden sticks. They looked like they were in a cast of a logger's version of *West Side Story*. They were ready to rumble.

I was mortified. "No, no! Go back to work!"

I shook my head. I was embarrassed by my behavior. I set the worst example I could have as a supervisor. I could have made my point with the official from the office without raising my voice. But my loggers were happy. From their perspective I was doing the right thing.

A few days later, another strike team leader who had just been assigned to my division said to me, "I don't know what's been going on here, but these loggers would follow you into hell." It gave me pause. It was a reminder of the lesson I already knew: you have to speak in the language of those you're leading. You can't talk to the loggers like you do to the mayor.

Before I left the fire after my three-week assignment, I got permission from the incident commander to get one night's sleep in a hotel. I had been coming down with a sore throat, and I knew if I could get one night's sleep in a bed off the damp ground, I might avert a weeklong illness. He agreed, and I went into town for a night in the only motel. One of the loggers found out I was going to spend the night in town and insisted I had to join the group for a beer at the town tavern.

Normally I wouldn't have done it, but these men and I had covered some ground together, from the first day they thought I was just a piece of feminine fluff from California to the day that they were ready to back me up in a fight. I went to join them for a beer.

When I walked in, the bar was jam-packed with locals. I felt like the conquering hero walking through the city gates. I couldn't buy my own beer. As a matter of fact, the bar had beer tokens that you could buy and give away to someone else. When you wanted a beer, the token served as payment. By the end of the night my pockets were literally overflowing with wooden beer tokens. I must have had fifty tokens, and they were falling out of every pocket in my pants and jacket. It was an interesting feeling. I felt a lot of camaraderie with those guys. I don't know how it would have been a few years before, but now as a female fire chief, I felt comfortable, I felt accepted, and I felt respected. It was a great feeling.

Before I left to go back to the motel, I sat quietly at the bar by myself. After a few minutes, I looked up at the wall, above the mirror behind the bar. There was a nicely carved and painted sign. In big letters it read NO QUEERS ALLOWED.

I laughed to myself, wondering what these tough characters would have said had they known my story. I had affection for them because we had covered a lot of ground over the previous weeks. And at the same time, I felt ambivalence and the tiniest bit of fear. Under different circumstances, might I have been in danger if this community had known my whole story?

11

THE SPIRIT LEADS

AFTER A FEW YEARS WORKING in California, my discomfort with the office dynamics encouraged me to look for greener pastures. A fire chief from a southern California county fire department told me about a couple of vacant positions in his department. He let me know that if I simply applied, with all my years of experience and education, I'd be sure to get a job as a battalion chief. I thought long and hard about applying. The pay was much better than a job with a federal wildland fire agency. But I was afraid of being back in the fire department environment. I was doing well working in the wildland fire service. Would I be as safe and successful working for another fire department?

Around the same time, I received a phone call from a national forest back in Washington State. They had remembered seeing my resume a couple years before thanks to my friend Steve. They asked me to apply for one of their vacant positions, and I told them that I would.

It was a tough decision for me. Do I go back to the Pacific Northwest to a town I had never seen, or move to Southern California, which was close to where I had grown up and was familiar to me? I had experienced discrimination and bullying at both the Forest Service and in fire departments. What was the right choice for me now? I made a critical life decision to go with a natural resource agency rather than a fire department. It was my intuition that led me back to the beautiful Pacific Northwest, or maybe it was the Holy Spirit.

While I was pondering my decision, the deadline to apply for the job in Washington passed. My hesitancy had decided for me, and I had mixed emotions. Should I have applied? It felt too late now.

Shortly after, I got a call from the supervisor in Washington. They didn't see my name on the list of applicants. They thought based on our previous conversation that I was going to apply for the job and were disappointed I hadn't. The process for the federal government system is that once you apply for a job, if you are a top candidate, you'll likely have a phone interview, and a couple weeks later, you'll find out if you got the job or not. In my case, I didn't apply, and by not deciding, a decision had been made.

A few weeks later, my assistant and I came in from the field and walked back into my office. The red light on my answering machine was flashing. I let the messages play on my machine while we talked. I was shocked to hear from the national forest in Washington—again. They had called to coordinate my "start date" for my new job.

What?! When was I going to start the new job up in Washington? I hadn't even applied for the job. There was no interview. The last I heard about that job was they were disappointed that I didn't apply. Now they were asking when I could start. I sat there in shock because after it was too late to apply, I had decided that I really should have applied.

I went home and cried. Not tears of joy or even tears of fear, but tears at the realization that all of a sudden, without any time to prepare emotionally, I was moving from a safe place to the unknown once again. When I said my prayers that night, I prayed for guidance as I continued on this path.

In the federal system, it's allowable to simply move an employee from one job to another or from one agency to another if both positions are at the same pay grade. In this case, I was at a different agency, but in the same pay grade. I was unaware of all the back-channel conversations that had been occurring within the national forest's personnel department and my future boss. But because of them, somehow, I was now starting a job I'd never even applied for.

In my life, I have had enough mysterious things happen to me that I quit believing in coincidences. I used to read and listen to recorded teachings by an Indian priest and psychotherapist by the name of Anthony de Mello. Father de Mello had a unique philosophy and perspective on Christian scripture. Not surprisingly, his teachings were eventually rejected by the Roman Catholic Church. I often return to this idea he explored:

> If you believe in coincidences instead of the Holy Spirit, when you make the Sign of the Cross, you should say, "In the name of the Father, the Son and the Holy Coincidence."

That quote makes me smile, but in many cases, I believe it is true.

How I made it back to the US Forest Service by way of Washington was unlikely at best. Working in California was an important step as well. While in California, I gained great insight into the workings of Cal Fire, which would be useful to me in the future. I responded to dozens of fires in areas I would have never seen before. I made deep friendships that were a balm to my soul. My move from the temporary fire department job in Washington, down to California, and then back up to Washington was pivotal for my career. I had no idea what lay ahead at the time, but looking back, my short California detour had been significant for my work and my emotional well-being.

In hindsight, my fire assignment working for Steve in eastern Oregon back in 1996 was pivotal in my career. After my divorce, I went on a search for a new job and a new life, and Steve connected me with Bob, the fire chief at a small fire department. Bob hired me as a contractor for a special project. Bob and Steve both made connections for me with the national forest in Washington. I worked for a couple years in California gaining great experience, and then in 2001 the national forest hired me without me even applying for the job. Here I was, back in the Pacific Northwest. Before I retired, I would have three more promotions as a result of Steve and Bob's ongoing friendship and support. From my perspective, this was way more than luck, and I try to be as grateful as I can be.

When I arrived in my new position in Washington, my employees were looking at me with some wariness, primarily because I was from

California, and to some degree because I was a female fire chief from California. In some parts of the country, especially back then, if you were a firefighter from California, you already had a strike against you. California firefighters are accused of having an attitude, though if they have an attitude, they've probably earned it. They see lots of fires, though things have changed in the last twenty years because now everyone in the West is experiencing the same kinds of fire behavior that those in California have been living through for decades.

In my twenty-seven-year career, I had only spent a couple of those years working in California. But when I showed up in a small Washington town snuggled at the base of the Cascade Mountains in my pretty, new red VW Beetle with California plates, the locals thought I was pure Californian.

I didn't realize what a big deal this was until one evening at an employee family picnic. The husband of one of the front office workers, who was a local farmer, came up to me and said, "Is that your car?" as he pointed at my red Beetle.

Proudly I said, "Yes, cool, huh? I love it."

He looked me dead in the eyes and said, "Girl, you had better get rid of those California plates."

I started laughing, thinking he was joking. But he didn't crack a smile. I quickly realized that I wasn't in Kansas anymore. I would have to be more aware that people were really watching me.

Being a female fire chief from California also presented a challenge for credibility. In the preceding years, lawsuits had been filed in California by women firefighters who claimed workplace gender discrimination against the US Forest Service. A legal consent decree in California was in place, requiring the US Forest Service to hire more women in fire leadership positions. Regardless of intent, it painted all women with the same brush. The common belief was if you were promoted into a Forest Service fire leadership position, the only reason you got the job was because you were female. I was suspect because I came from California and was female. The irony was not lost on me. I didn't even work for the US Forest Service when I was in California, but it didn't matter. I had three strikes against me when I showed up in this quaint little mountain community. I didn't drive a pickup truck, I was female, and I came from California.

Most of my employees were born and raised in the local area. They all knew each other, and they all knew each other's family secrets. It was a town of immigrants from all over Europe. Although they were all at least second generation, the traditions lived on. It was fun to be a part of the community, but in a tight-knit little town, when one person hurts, everyone hurts.

Of the thirty-five or so firefighters who worked for me, there were four brothers from the same family. One of the brothers had recently taken a position at a neighboring ranger station. On July 10, 2001, his crew was overrun by a wildfire, and four firefighters died. He was one of them.

Early in the morning of July 11, I called a meeting of the entire district—including the nonfire personnel. This tragic news would affect everyone at the station for the rest of their life. I'll never forget standing in front of fifty or so employees and having to break the news that we had lost four firefighters from the neighboring ranger station, and one of them was their beloved Tom. There were audible gasps in the room. Several of the women from the office ran out of the meeting room sobbing. Many of the employees had watched Tom grow up in this small town. Everyone was in shock. His large family was well known in the small community, and Tom had been a football star in high school and at the nearby state college.

I had only arrived in my position in May, and it was now July. I barely had time to get the basics of the new job and district figured out, and now I had to deal with a workforce that was incapacitated by grief and my own baggage from the fatalities in the Dude Fire eleven years before.

Everyone has a different reaction when a tragedy like this happens. For me, I had flashbacks of the Dude Fire. I became angry. Anger, I realized, is how I dealt with the loss of life from a fire. I become mad at the agency, mad at the supervisors, mad at society for allowing young people to be put at such risk. Just mad.

Others at the station became oddly quiet and withdrew completely. One of my captains was so depressed he didn't come to work for days.

I finally drove to his home to talk to him. He came out of his house, and we sat on his front steps in the shade of the towering pine trees. Like everyone at the station, he had known Tom for years, and he came away with survivor's guilt. Sounds odd, doesn't it? He wasn't even at the fire and hadn't even worked with Tom for more than six months, but he was carrying guilt.

That's how post-traumatic stress works. You don't even have to be involved. It's like a cold; you can catch it from a distance. It doesn't have to make sense; it just is.

The summer progressed, and I settled into my new job. There were some personnel challenges, but I wore my cloak of confidence and dealt with each as it arose. There had been poor to no leadership before I arrived, so when I expected a certain level of performance and professionalism, there was some pushback as we created a new department culture. Generally, my firefighters were hardworking and adjusted to my expectations and standards, and eventually we developed a good esprit de corps. But soon our fire season would take another tragic turn that would change everyone's lives.

We all remember where we were and what we were doing on September 11, 2001. I was like everyone else. I was at home putting on my uniform for work as I watched the news of the attacks in New York City. I drove to the station because I knew things were going to change for us. I had firefighters assigned to fires in Montana and Idaho at the time of the attacks. My remaining firefighters were at the station, protecting our district. Soon I learned that the federal wildland fire agencies would be sending personnel to assist in Washington, DC, and New York City.

Many might be surprised to learn that the US Forest Service and the other federal wildland fire agencies respond to national emergencies as a part of the National Response Plan. The Federal Emergency Management Agency (FEMA) tasks each agency to assist in a national emergency when appropriate. There are preassigned missions for federal agencies based on their expertise. But back in 2001, there wasn't yet a National Response Framework. That would come years later as a result of 9/11. It quickly became clear that the wildland fire agencies had experience at organizing and directing firefighters during long-term emergencies. We had been doing it for years.

In firefighting, incident management teams (IMTs) are an organized group of fifty or more personnel with expertise in logistics, planning, finance/administration, and operations, along with safety and public information, all led by an incident commander. By the afternoon of September 12, several IMTs were being flown on charter jets to New York City and Washington, DC. The most highly qualified IMTs are classified as a type 1 team. I had been on incident management teams in the past, but I had not yet been assigned to one since my move.

All flights nationwide were grounded shortly after the morning attacks. That included the helicopters and air tankers on fires. I had crews assigned to fires out of state, and they had to sit where they were on the fire because the helicopters scheduled to pick them up were told to stand down.

We had minimum staffing levels at the station, which required either me or my assistant to be on duty or on call. That left one of us available at all times to respond to off-district fires with our IMTs. When the fog and confusion from those first days started to clear, I knew more IMTs were likely to be called up to the sites of the attacks. When I finally thought about it, I called my forest fire chief. He was a planning section chief on one of the IMTs that happened to be next up in the rotation to respond.

I called him and told him I wanted to go with his team if they got called up to New York City. I would do whatever I had to in order to help. He worked in the planning section. I was a firefighter; I worked in operations. In all my years I had never worked in anything other than operations. So when he asked me if I had any planning qualifications, I lied and said, "No, but I've always wanted to work in plans."

I really had no interest in working in the planning section. Anything other than being on the fire line and fighting fires seemed so unimportant to me. I always wanted to be where the fire or incident was most active, not in an office working on a plan.

Every firefighter in the country wanted to be in New York City or DC, and I was no different. I had to go. I had to help. A few days later, when my chief's team got called up, I tagged along as someone to work in the planning section. It was a white lie for the greater good.

Bob was the fire chief I had worked for in Washington, who hired me as a consultant for his fire department. Coincidentally, he was also the deputy incident commander on the IMT going to New York. He knew I wasn't truly interested in working in the planning section. When we arrived in New York, all the guys working in operations were going to head down to Ground Zero to reconnoiter and determine how we would implement the task given to us by the city of New York and FEMA.

Bob was going to accompany the operations section on the trip from the theater district where we were staying down to Ground Zero. He said to the planning section chief, "I'm going to take Bobbie with the ops folks down to the Trade Center."

The planning section chief's reply was fast and absolute, "No way! She agreed to come here to work in plans, not operations."

Bob responded, "Oh yeah, absolutely. It will just give her a better perspective on what's going on down there and will help out the entire planning process. She'll start working in plans tomorrow."

I spent that day with the operations guys, and I never once went back to the planning section. I spent the next twenty-nine days working at Ground Zero. God bless Bob and the Holy Coincidence.

Our IMT's mission was to support the city's logistical efforts at Ground Zero, the radius encompassing the World Trade Center complex and the attack site. At the center of Ground Zero was the Pile, the skeletons of steel and rubble where both towers had stood just days before. Our job was to acquire whatever tools and supplies were needed on the Pile for the police officers and firefighters on-site, and manage and disperse those resources. The operations section managed our IMT's work at the Pile, and we were supported by the rest of the IMT, who did the ordering of supplies, and set up and managed an 88,000-square-foot warehouse, along with a plethora of other tasks.

There were three primary city agencies involved in the rescue efforts when we arrived—and it was still a rescue mission. Rescue implies there are live people that you're trying to rescue, which means that time is critical. We are likely to take bigger personal risks to our safety to save others. Recovery means recovering the bodies of the deceased. It's a big difference. The Fire Department of the City of New York (FDNY), the City of New York Police Department (NYPD), and the Port Authority Police Department (PAPD) were providing their own logistical support to each of their own agency's personnel at the scene.

Our task was to assume logistical management of all the tools, equipment, and personal protective equipment (PPE) that was coming into the scene, as well as all the donated items such as boots, gloves, and socks, and supply them as needed to the workers on the Pile. In addition to the PPE, we ordered and distributed rolls of black plastic, rescue harnesses, rebar cutters, heavy-duty multipurpose saws, and much more. They were all needed for the firefighters, police officers, and steelworkers who were an integral part of the operation.

FDNY had their supply cache located in what had been a deli next to their Station 10. Station 10 was located on Liberty Street directly across from the South Tower and the Marriott hotel. I was assigned to work with the firefighters operating their supply cache and talk them into allowing our IMT to build a twenty-four-foot-by-twenty-four-foot temporary building out on the street, as well as convince them to let us manage it.

That wasn't going to be an easy task.

I was overwhelmed by a visceral feeling of death at that station. Two-thirds of the firefighters assigned to Station 10 had been on duty that morning. The attacks occurred during shift change, meaning there were firefighters coming to work and firefighters leaving to go home. Twice as many firefighters were on duty than would normally be at the station. Five of those firefighters would perish that morning They hadn't even recovered the engine or ladder truck yet. Ladder 10 wouldn't be found for weeks and was still buried somewhere under forty feet of rubble, swallowed up into the abyss that surrounded the South Tower.

I was directed to talk to the firefighters who were staffing their supply cache next door in what looked like a bombed-out deli. The front windows had been busted out by the blast when the South Tower came down. The same dust that surrounded the collapsed towers covered the streets blocks away, piles of it more than eight inches deep, coating everything. Firefighters had been trudging through and living in that horrible dust for days.

One day, when I was taking a breather and looking at the Pile and thinking about the towers, I wondered where all the concrete went. A cursory calculation on my part figured that there had to be at least two hundred acres of concrete scattered about. That's just the concrete from the floors of both towers. That didn't include the concrete used for elevator shafts and other reinforcements.

I'm not an engineer, and I know little about the construction of the Twin Towers, but if each building had been about one acre in size and one hundred stories tall, minimally there should be about two hundred acres of broken concrete lying around in chunks and pieces. Instead, what I saw was dust. Thick dust everywhere. And I can only assume each concrete floor had fireproofing sprayed on its underside to provide protection from fires. When the towers were built, I would bet that much of that sprayed-on insulation had asbestos in it. I watched these firefighters wade through this dust every day, a cloud trailing behind them. I knew it wasn't good, but it would be years before we would discover just how harmful it was. That dust would prove deadly for many in the years to come.

I tried to talk to the firefighters about letting me deal with all the equipment and PPE, but they were numb. They were like zombies lumbering through their makeshift supply cache. I was respectful and I was considerate, but I tried to make my case that they really shouldn't be working or living in that hazardous environment.

"You know, there's probably all sorts of hazardous materials in this dust," I said. "Probably asbestos."

They looked back at me with a faraway stare. "You think so?"

"Yeah, I do," I said. "You guys should get out of here and let us take over the supply function."

They didn't have that many tools or supplies in their cache. Mostly it was a pile of picks and shovels. But they weren't going to leave their post, and I wasn't going to argue with them. Instead, we started construction of a wood-frame building with a big plastic tarp roof. It was just thirty yards down the street from Station 10 and the deli. Once it was built and I started bringing in more equipment, they slowly left the deli. It was horribly sad to watch. I will never forget the blank looks on their faces. They had lost so many friends and coworkers. I wonder, how are they now? Are they healthy or sick? It's hard not to worry about them.

I saw no other women working at the Pile. There were women volunteers serving drinks and food, such as coffee and donuts. There were women at the Red Cross tent, but I saw no women working on the Pile. I now know there were some there, but I never saw them. Because there were so few women firefighters working at Ground Zero, and I was there every day, I might have stood out.

I had a friend named Pete* who was an FDNY captain. We spoke through e-mails after the attacks, and I knew he was safe, but he had not heard from his two sons who were also FDNY firefighters and were on duty the morning of the attacks. The last communication we had before I traveled to New York was through e-mail, since communications had been so disjointed following the attacks. I told him I was on my way to New York City but had no idea where I would be working. Once I arrived, my days were busy, and I had forgotten to let him know where I was.

One day while I was hard at work in my building at the corner of Church and Liberty streets, the door swung open.

It was Pete.

"I knew it had to be you!" he yelled out. "One of my guys came back to my fire engine and said, 'Some bitch is running that supply cache.'"

He came over and gave me a big bear hug. I saw a friendly face and felt better. He let me know that he finally spoke to his sons and they had made it out safely.

Never having been to New York City before, I wasn't used to how New Yorkers spoke. I didn't know their language. I grew up unaccustomed to much cursing; I rarely heard the word "fuck." So I was surprised to hear it dropped continuously through the day. It didn't matter if a cop was describing a "fucking good pizza," or a firefighter

---

* Pseudonym

was wanting a "fucking hoodie." At the time I didn't even know what a hoodie was, let alone a "fucking good" one. Being in New York made me feel like a Minnie Pearl character. I wanted to say, "Ooh-ie, look at all those lights and tall buildings!" But I wasn't Minnie Pearl. I was an experienced firefighter with an equivalent rank to one of FDNY's battalion chiefs. And here I was working on the street across from the Pile, talking to cops, firefighters, and steelworkers.

Often I was just talked *at*. "Hey, honey, I need some bolt cutters." "Hey, cutie, I need another pair of gloves." Or the one where I lost it: "Hey, sweetie, I need a fucking hoodie." I had been called "sweetie" about two thousand times by the first responders, and the first responder requesting the hoodie was twenty years younger and many ranks below me. I exploded. Adopting the local vernacular, I said in my loudest fire chief voice, "Get the fuck out of here!" while forcefully pointing at the door.

"Do you talk to your battalion chief that way?" I kept going. "Don't fucking come back in here until you can speak to me with the same respect you show your battalion chief. Now get the fuck out!"

I was wildly angry.

What I hadn't noticed in my blacked-out f-bomb rage was that my incident commander (IC) along with several executives from the Washington, DC, Forest Service headquarters had walked into the cache, catching me in the middle of my verbal spew. As the young firefighter skulked out the door, my eyes caught the new visitors standing in the doorway. My IC cleared his throat, rolled his eyes, and made the introductions. He was clearly and obviously unhappy with me. One of the executives was the deputy fire director for the entire US Forest Service and would go on to become the national fire director. Little did I know, he was someone who would have a direct impact on my future career. He seemed to enjoy the show, a slight grin on his face, while I wanted to wither away of embarrassment.

There were some benefits to being a female fire chief working at Ground Zero, although they didn't feel like benefits at the time. A week or so after we got the new supply cache set up and running, I was switched to night shift. We had been working twelve-hour shifts. Being scheduled for twelve hours really meant fourteen, between the time you arrived at Ground Zero and the time you left, trekking back and forth to the hotel. Ultimately, we ended up working sixteen-hour shifts due to the daily deluge of unexpected issues and events. This left just enough time to take a shower, get six hours of sleep, and go back the next day.

When I changed to night shift, it was like the whole world had changed.

Everyone has seen photos of the Pile after 9/11, the towering, twisted, broken steel structures sticking out of the rubble. Huge spotlights had been set up on the streets around the perimeter lighting up the Pile. Smoke soared up toward the sky and into the darkness, and out of the smoke dropped pieces of ash and dust. With the lights shining, it looked like it was snowing all night long. The same dust and debris were raining down out of the smoke during the day, but you couldn't really see them. At night, I realized how much I had been breathing in.

All the firefighters, cops, and ironworkers working on and around the Pile had been fitted for and issued a respirator. We were supposed to use it while working around the Pile to avoid breathing in all the dust and toxins floating about in the air. We knew we were breathing dangerous materials, but no one wore their respirator other than the occasional Occupational Safety and Health Administration (OSHA) inspector keeping an eye on things.

I've always been safety conscious at work. I've prided myself in being smart, being safe, and making sure those around me were too. But I didn't wear my respirator one time after getting fitted for it when we arrived in New York. At the time it seemed irrelevant.

The New York City Emergency Operations Center (EOC) had been in the basement at the World Trade Center. It was destroyed in the collapse of the towers. Following the attacks, the city moved their EOC to an empty wharf building on the Hudson River. The first time I went to the EOC, there were huge snowplow dump trucks surrounding the front of the building. Large machine guns were mounted in the back of the trucks, to protect the city's EOC. Military jets patrolled the skies. In the days and weeks that followed, when people heard or saw a jet overhead, they paused to look up, wondering if there was another attack under way.

One day, I was able to take a few hours off during the daylight. I decided to experience a true New York City deli. While sitting next to the window eating my first real deli sandwich, I watched the hustle and bustle of the city going by me. Everything seemed normal, but at the sound of a distant siren coming from the streets, the energy changed. The crowd slowed down and started to nervously look around. Everyone was on guard. Multiple fire engines and police vehicles screeched to a halt outside a building across from the deli. Police and fire personnel donned hazardous materials suits and ran inside. This was becoming a common scene. At the time, anthrax was being sent to offices as threats. Ultimately many were hoaxes, but the fear in the city was real.

Wearing a respirator seemed so insignificant to me at the time. Why would I bother to wear my respirator in order to protect my health for some unknown future? What's the point of worrying about my future health when it seemed that nothing would ever be the same? We were at war and waiting for the next attack. The world had changed and would never be as it once was. Safety didn't seem nearly so important.

When I started working night shift, the big generator-powered lights in the street were shining on the Pile. The cranes stuck out all around as workers climbed, digging through the Pile. It looked surreal. It was like looking at a movie set, smoke rising up from the Pile, the lights making it opaque. It was a different place than it had been during the day.

During the day, I made the rounds to the different "sectors" to check in with the on-duty fire division chief or police commander, to see if there were any needs or let them know a piece of equipment they had ordered arrived. The individual firefighters, police personnel, and steelworkers would come in for one thing or another, like tools and PPE. But at night, some of them behaved differently.

I can remember many times when I was standing across the street from the Pile in the shadows. You couldn't stand in the middle of the street for too long. There were still glass shards falling from the broken windows of the tall buildings surrounding what had been the World Trade Center towers. Wooden covers had been built over the sidewalks next to all the buildings to protect you from the dangers of all the falling glass. So, you either stayed next to the building under the cover of the wood structure, or you moved closer to the Pile, away from the falling glass.

It was dark across the street from the Pile because the big spotlights were aimed in the opposite direction. Anyone standing back away from the street and the Pile would be partially hidden in the dark. By now, many of the emergency workers had seen me often enough that I had become a familiar face to them. And at night, in the shadows, they began to tell me their stories: What they had experienced, what they had survived. They were horrible stories. After more than twenty-five years of firefighting, I had experienced plenty of trauma myself. I had seen dead bodies. Victims died in my arms. I'd seen the exposed broken bones and heard the screams of pain and terror at accident scenes. I never talked much about my memories to anyone; I buried these thoughts, hoping to ignore them. But the stories the New York City firefighters and cops told me at night were so hideous, so traumatic, that they conjure up nightmarish images I still can't shake.

Witnessing such horror changes you—forever. I wasn't at the World Trade Center during the tower collapses. I didn't see the horror that the firefighters and cops did, but when they described what they lived through, it was almost like they were saying, "Tag, you're it." A piece of that memory now lived with me; what they described was etched into my mind. They didn't mean to cause me any problems, and, really, I was honored to be there for them to talk to. But what they told me will stay in my mind's eye forever, never to be shared with anyone.

I noticed that none of my male coworkers were having the same experience. No one came up to my male coworkers in the shadows at night to describe the horror they witnessed. I believe that my being a woman gave the emergency workers a sense of comfort; they felt safe to unburden themselves. My experience as a female fire chief was different from the men I worked alongside. I was honored to be there for them, and I was thankful.

In mid-2020, the number of firefighter deaths attributed to cancer and related illness following 9/11 had reached 227. That is in addition to the 343 firefighter deaths that occurred when the towers collapsed. Symptoms attributed to exposure to the dust include chronic cough, shortness of breath, sinus infections, certain cancers, and related disorders. I'm under medical care myself, for a chronic cough I developed after 9/11.

And it wasn't just the dust from the collapse. It was also the smoke. When the towers collapsed, they were on fire. Those fires burned for ninety-nine days following the attack. The fires were burning when I arrived, and they were still burning when I left almost a month later. As the fires burned, smoke filled with the dust, and microparticles continued to be entrained in the smoke column, falling to the ground around the Pile. Falling onto us.

12

FINDING SOLID GROUND

BACK AT MY LITTLE MOUNTAIN home in Washington, I installed a little white-picket fence with an arbor in the front yard. I was so proud watching the flowers bloom, the climbing roses growing over the arbor. It gave me a sense of calm to have my modest little home and flower gardens. It was my safety zone. During the frigid snow-filled winters, I snuggled up to the woodstove and felt gratitude and loneliness at the same time.

My years working in that little mountain community in Washington were a blessing to me in so many ways. My successes at work helped me develop more self-confidence, not only professionally, but also personally. My work, my profession, was how I really grew. It made up for, at least a little bit, my loss of family. Without my career and the excitement and satisfaction that came with it, I would have been lost. As it was, I was proud of my work and my career and that meant something considering everything I had been through. A few years earlier, I'd had no job and no money and had felt like a lost soul. In the intervening years, I had grown both personally and professionally. I owned my own home, I was able to pay my child support, I had friends, and felt like I was successful in so many ways. That little mountain community was a marker on my life's journey. It showed me that even if life was painful and at times difficult, I was so fortunate. I had a great job that I loved as a district fire management officer / division chief. I was finally back on my feet financially and bought a little home. It was a tiny starter home, but it was mine—and the bank's. I even had my own washer and dryer. No more trips to the laundromat. These simple things made me feel rich. They made me feel normal and ordinary. After five years of living on the edge, I was finally starting to feel more secure.

I had made friends through work, but I was very guarded in those relationships, and I hadn't met too many people outside of the work environment. I didn't feel open to getting too close to anyone I had a work connection with. I would never lie if someone asked me about my past, but no one ever did.

In all the years in my career, no one ever asked, "So, is it true that you changed your gender?" No one ever said, "I've heard some stories about you; would you mind if I ask some questions?"

If someone had asked, I would have been honest about it. But I wasn't going to make a big, unexpected announcement about my past either. And I think most people were just as happy to not know any details. In fact, many people might not have known anything at all about my past. I have no idea who knew what. But when you can't—or feel you can't—share personal things about yourself, the relationships tend to stay at a shallow level. Without real personal intimacy, a meaningfully close friendship isn't possible.

On the professional side of life, I was doing well. I devoted myself to my work. My employees adapted to my expectations, and I probably softened a bit of my hard edge after a year or two. The more confident I was of earning their trust and respect in me as their leader, the less tough and hard-core I had to be. Things got done the way I wanted, so there was little reason to be hard on my firefighters and supervisors.

As odd as it may sound, the fires were awesome. People who aren't emergency responders might not get it, but I loved going to a fire—and we had a lot of fires. Firefighters *want* to fight fires. We want to feel useful, and saving a house, a town, or a life is an incredible way to accomplish something meaningful.

While I was working in my small community, an arsonist was also at work. We began to have some serious fires burn where most of the towns and rural subdivisions were. He was eventually caught, but in the meantime he brought a lot of fire business to the valley.

My jurisdiction was higher up the mountains above town, farther from all the developments in the valley. We surrounded some of the more remote communities, but the low country where most of the population lived was protected by the state of Washington and the many smaller county fire departments. When a fire was spreading rapidly and lives and homes were imperiled, it was all hands on deck. All the agencies responded.

One day, a fire started in a rural area of the valley and was burning toward a subdivision surrounded by miles of brush and scattered trees. The winds were howling that afternoon, and the fire was moving quickly. The homes in this subdivision were located on large one- to two-acre lots, so there was plenty of flammable vegetation between the homes. Every home had piles of firewood or sheds filled with combustible materials and piles of junk behind them. The grass and brush were thick, and if the fire reached the subdivision, we would lose many homes and possibly some lives. It was a critical situation.

I didn't wait for a formal request and immediately sent one of my fire engines down valley to lend a hand to the small volunteer fire department. It sounded hectic on the radio—not a good sign. I didn't respond immediately because in mutual-aid situations you normally wait to be requested—even though I had already sent one of my engines without asking. I knew the fire chief, and I knew he'd appreciate the help. After only a few more minutes listening to the radio conversations, I began to get concerned. I got on the fire department's radio frequency from my office, called the chief, and asked if he wanted me to respond. His reply made it clear that he needed help, "Get here right away; I need you now!"

OK, the situation was as serious as it sounded on the radio.

It was about ten miles down a two-lane highway that ran through a steep picturesque canyon. Scenic cliffs bordered the road on one side, and a popular fly-fishing river was on the other. The incident command post where I would find the local chief was near where the cliffs opened up to the wider valley. When I arrived, the local state of Washington fire chief was just arriving. From listening to the radio traffic on the way to the fire, I knew this fire had the potential to be very bad.

As I walked up to the chief and my state counterpart, I said, "What can I do, Chief? Where do you want me?"

The chief was wound up, a bit anxious. "You take operations!"

He wanted me to be the operations chief on this fire. It would be a bit stressful. As the ops chief, I would be responsible for directing all the fire engines, firefighters, bulldozer, aircraft, and other firefighting resources on the fire. The only problem was the fire was moving extremely fast, and the subdivision was in the direct path of the fire. In addition, I had no idea how many firefighters and fire engines were already on scene and where they were located. There had been no organizing of the fire resources yet. There were no strike team leaders or division supervisors assigned or on scene either. I was the only supervisor at a fire scene with more than a dozen fire engines, a bulldozer, helicopters, and air tankers. I could see the flashing red lights from the fire engines scattered about at the residences, preparing to protect the homes when the fire overran the subdivision. There was only one way in and one way out of the subdivision—and that road would soon be engulfed by the fast-moving fire. It felt inevitable.

If I had been in different circumstances, I would have found my best crew, given them a briefing about what I'd like them to do, and developed a plan to conduct a backfire on the road. The backfire would stop the fire from burning all the homes in the path of the fire. I was the ops chief, and I should have been directing and supervising, but I had no time to organize the firefighting resources on scene. I had to make sure that homes and lives were not lost in the next hour.

There was a state fire engine on the road nearest the fire, and I told the captain I needed one of his firefighters to come with me. The young man who was directed to follow me was a fresh recruit. It was his first fire season on the job. He was very inexperienced, but he was enthusiastic and ready to help. I gave him a half-dozen firefighting fuzees. A fuzee is like a road flare but longer. It is one tool out of many that can be used for starting burn-outs and backfires. I directed him to start burning the grass and brush with the fuzees along the road opposite the side with the houses. He walked about ten or fifteen feet from and parallel to the road on the side where the fire was coming from, upwind of the road, lighting the tall grass and brush with his fuzee as he went. The fires he lit produced flames of about four or five feet tall. Because there was only a short distance between where he lit the fuel and the road, the fire didn't have a chance to build up much energy, reducing the reach of the flames. The main fire had flame heights of fifty to one hundred feet tall. Our backfire was much more manageable.

While the firefighter started the backfire, I walked farther in off the road in between the backfire and the main fire burning toward us. I walked parallel, in the same direction as the firefighter, but I was about one hundred feet in from the road. I started a similar firing operation. My burn-out had approximately fifty feet or more to burn before it ran into the firefighter's burn-out. Now we had turned the road and all our burned-out fuel into a one-hundred-foot-wide firebreak, in anticipation of the oncoming wildfire that was gaining strength and heading our way.

While we were conducting the backfire, I called several fire engines down from the houses to patrol the road to keep any spot fires from jumping our widened fire line. In order to add more depth to our burn-out and keep the head of the wildfire from jumping our lines, I pulled out every wildland firefighter's favorite tool.

In my pack I kept what looked like a regular revolver pistol. It is called a Very Pistol. It uses .22 caliber blanks to propel small fuzees 100 to 150 feet to start more fires, aiding in the backfire strategy. I used the handheld fuzees to start fires as I walked along, and every fifty feet or so, I'd fire off a couple rounds from the pistol to add to the depth of our backfire operation. We walked about a mile, burning the vegetation with the fuzees and the pistol, all while keeping a close eye on the oncoming wildfire.

If I had been using experienced firefighters with a well-thought-out plan, this operation would have been considered very risky. But a young, inexperienced, yet eager, firefighter and I were the only ones involved—and my recruit didn't know just how at risk we were. If we failed, many of the homes in the subdivision would likely be lost. And due to the narrowness of the roads and the surrounding thick vegetation creating a heavy fuel supply, the firefighters themselves would be at risk of being burned over.

Thankfully and according to plan, when the main wildfire collided with our backfire, it fizzled out. The fast-moving wildfire laid right down when it hit the burn-out.

It was a perfect example of fighting fire with fire.

The subdivision was safe thanks to a calculated risk. Had things not turned out the way they did, I would have been accused of a crazy, ill-thought-out tactic. As it turned out, I looked heroic. But things could have gone very badly. If we would have had a spot fire jump our lines, we could have lost the subdivision—or worse. But there had been no time to hesitate. Swift action was called for, and I'm grateful things went well. The subsequent flanks of the fire were knocked down using a bulldozer and a heavy air tanker. When the fire was secured, I turned it back to the local fire chief and drove home for a shower and some relaxation after the exciting, adrenaline-filled afternoon.

Fire engines from surrounding cities one hundred miles away arrived to find the fire had already been knocked down. They were surprised to see the fire just smoldering. All they had left to do was mop up the hotspots and patrol the perimeter overnight. When I stopped by the fire in the morning on the way to my station, the firefighters from the distant cities were on duty finishing up their assignment. They gave me a good-natured ribbing.

"All we heard when we got here was, 'Scopa put out the fire. You should have seen her. Scopa started a huge backfire, and the fire went out,'" they said.

The local firefighters hadn't seen a backfire used this way. All my burning experience had paid dividends. It made me laugh to be teased by my friends with the larger fire departments. In some ways, that fire made me feel like I had arrived.

Even though I always acted confident and had been successful on the job, a lifetime of worrying about what people thought of me or were thinking about me caused me to second-guess my decisions and communications. But this fire as well as others during the same time period gave me real confidence and fortified my professional self-esteem. Not only did I believe I knew my job and could perform under pressure but also others thought so too. It had been my own insecurities working against me. I already had enough experience and history. Anyone else would have walked with a swagger. But I wasn't anyone else. I didn't swagger, but I did have confidence, which was way better.

The more fires I fought, the more I loved my job. When my professional self-esteem improved, it was almost like the overflow self-esteem filled my personal self-esteem. In the past, a high professional sense of self didn't at all correlate to a high level of personal confidence. But now, my successes as a fire chief and firefighter were making me more confident as a person. Earlier in my career while working at the fire department, those around me would have considered my career a success. I was often promoted quickly and was a leader. But due to my internal conflict over my gender, that success never translated into my personal self-esteem. Back then, I spent too much energy worrying about losing my cover, worrying about what others were thinking about me. But this was different. Now I wasn't worried about what people were thinking or saying about me. It didn't matter. My overflow of self-confidence and job satisfaction was having an impact on my personal and emotional well-being.

After returning to Washington from my time at Ground Zero, I had been assigned to my own incident management team. It would be the first time since my transition and move that I would be on an IMT. It was the month of April, and all the IMTs were having their team meetings. I didn't know anyone on the team that I had been assigned to; I was showing up cold. The meetings were being held at a local convention center about fifty miles from my station. There would be nearly four hundred people in total attending the meetings for the five different teams, including all the administrators and others.

I was waiting in the hallway outside the door that said "WA IMT 4." I was a bit nervous since I didn't know anyone, and I was there as their new operations section chief. It's a responsible and visible position on the team. On a fire, all the firefighters work for the ops chief, and the ops chief works for the incident commander. It's an important position.

While I was waiting in the hallway for all the team members— probably seventy in all, including alternates and trainees—a gentleman approached and asked if I was a new member of IMT 4. I said yes and just smiled.

He asked, "What section are you working in, plans?"

"No," I replied. "Not plans."

"Oh, logistics? You're working in logistics?"

I didn't want this to get more uncomfortable. "No, not logistics. I'm the new operations chief."

He looked at me oddly. He shook his head and said, "Oh, I don't know about this, I don't know about this at all . . . a female ops chief?"

I stood there, smiling to myself at all the layers of this conversation. If I were another person, a stronger person, or if it were another time, we could have had an interesting discussion. But it didn't feel like the right moment.

After a few minutes of awkward silence, he said, "I'm sorry, but I spent several tours in Vietnam, and I've seen a lot of bad stuff in combat. And you know, firefighting can be a bit like combat. My dad raised me to protect women, and I just don't know how I feel about this."

At once, I wanted to hit him across his head and give him a hug. I could see the emotional weight of what he was carrying around with him from Vietnam. But his attitude was exactly what I had been pushing against for years. I didn't know it at the time, but he and I would grow to be friends. He was bighearted and a wonderful human being.

Over the next few years, my incident management team would respond to many fires across the western United States. But on this day, we were assigned to a fire in eastern Wyoming. We had been quite successful assisting the county fire department in suppressing multiple lightning fires in their jurisdiction. There had been some concern by the county fire department that this outside team of "federales," as they called us, was going to come in and step on the toes of all the local citizens and leave a public-relations mess or be too inept to even put out their fires. They obviously had had some negative experiences with out-of-state IMTs.

The culture of our team was to be as helpful and humble as possible—and that's not always easy for a bunch of type A knuckle-dragging firefighters. As a team, we performed well, and we were feeling a bit full of ourselves when it was all over. The line from *Ghostbusters* always came to mind in circumstances like this, "We came, we saw, we kicked its ass." We were badass firefighters.

About a week after our arrival in eastern Wyoming, the fire was out, and we were driven to Rapid City to catch commercial flights back to home. Empty seats on the flights were scarce, so most of the operations folks (the firefighting types as opposed to the logistics, plans, and finance workers) were sitting in the airport bar sipping on beers and telling stories, hoping we'd get a flight out that day. That afternoon, as we told tall tales about our firefighting adventures and drank beer, the stories began to veer away from firefighting into other areas of our lives.

I had and still have great affection for this group of guys. At the time, I was the only woman among them, and I was one of two ops chiefs on that fire that shared supervision of them. This group had been working together for a while; we'd established a great rapport and a high level of mutual respect. If I had been insecure when I joined the group a year before, I was comfortable among my brothers now.

Everyone's favorite person in the group was the senior ops chief. On the organization chart, he and I were equals, but in terms of seniority and respect, Mark was above me. We shared responsibility for running the operations section, and I loved working with Mark. We both had positional power because of our roles as the ops chiefs. But Mark also had informal power due to his experience and personality.

When things were busy and serious, Mark was all business. He wore his role of leader like a grand robe around his shoulders. And he had a booming voice that fit the magnitude of his role. He could use that voice like thunder when necessary, but he never overused it. I never felt intimidated by or less than Mark or those who worked for us because I was new to the team or the only woman. It was great fun working with and being around Mark.

We were all just a bit loosened up by a beer or two in that South Dakota airport bar. I was telling as many stories as Mark, and everyone was laughing and having a good time. I was reveling in the camaraderie of my fellow firefighters and feeling safe among them. Someone finally asked Mark how he liked living in Portland, Oregon, since he had moved from a small Idaho town to the US Forest Service regional office. Mark started telling tall tales of living in the big, liberal city of Portland. He switched between serious to funny stories, and everyone listened as they sipped on their beer.

Finally, he said, "Ya know, riding the train into work every day is really an adventure. You never know what you're going to see." In his booming country twang he continued, "Why just last week, I saw one of them *he-shes*, and she must have just gotten a new set of boobs because she was strutting around and showing off for everyone to see."

Everyone laughed and talked about how Portland really was weird and you never knew what you were going to see. I listened to my good friend, not knowing if I should say anything and if I did, what it would be. I sat there feeling like a Judas.

Finally, I said, "Well, you never know what is going on in people's lives."

It was a weak response. Should I say more in front of the folks who work for me and Mark? Should I wait and say something to Mark in private? What should I say? Should I say to him, "Hey Mark, you know, I'm transgender too. Technically, I used to be a man."

But I never said anything else. And no one looked at me or acted differently. It confirmed for me that at least on that day, not one of my firefighting brothers knew about my past. It gave me a feeling of reprieve, but also a feeling of regret. It was an opportunity lost.

My relationship with Mark only grew stronger. We continued to work together, and we developed a real affection for each other. He was a great guy, and I enjoyed every fire assignment we worked together. We told each other stories, and I laughed more with Mark than I have with anyone else. Over the years, I kept promising myself that one of these days I was going to tell him. I thought maybe if he knew about me, he'd be more sensitive to others living their lives who weren't able to—or didn't want to—blend in. It reinforced how fortunate I had been, but I was still hiding.

We both retired around the same time. He and his wife moved back to the mountains of Idaho, and we stayed in touch about once a year. My plan was to accept an invitation from Mark and his wife to come visit them on their little farm. When I was there, I would sit alone with Mark and tell him about my past. Maybe by now he already knew. He probably did. But I felt I had to make up for the time he had made an offhand comment about a transgender woman and I had said nothing. I needed to educate my beloved friend.

Unfortunately, the summer before my planned visit, Mark died. His passing affected everyone who knew him: his wife, son, and sisters, and so many friends. I was sad not only at the loss of a great friend, but also because I was never completely honest with Mark about who I was. I wanted to tell him not because of a need to shame him or make him feel bad about what he had said those decades ago, but rather because it's hard to be truly close to someone if they don't know who you are. Mark and I shared a camaraderie that can only come from the shared trauma and experiences of our work, and a true friendship grew out of that bond. He gave me so much warmth and confidence, yet a little bit of disquietude too. It breaks my heart that my good friend died before I could let him know about me. His friendship wouldn't have faltered—I'm sure of it.

But as time continues to pass, it's a tough reminder: I don't want to hide myself from my closest friends.

13

LOOKING FOR LOVE

AFTER MY DIVORCE, BUT BEFORE I had fully transitioned and had my gender surgery, dating might have seemed like a complicated or even dangerous endeavor. How could I date a man if I hadn't yet had gender surgery? I'd feel disingenuous, and more important, potentially at physical risk.

Yet following my divorce, my social life got busy. I was active in the "divorced, widowed, and singles" group through church. Our church group met with the singles groups from other churches as well. We played volleyball and cards, went to the movies together, attended church Bible studies, and began to form a comfortable friendship.

From all appearances, I was just another divorced woman in our group—even though I had not yet had gender surgery. No one knew what was or wasn't in my pants. The subject never came up, ever. After a volleyball game or an evening playing cards with our mixed group of singles, if a guy asked me if I wanted to go to a movie or to the local dirt-track car races or out for a cup of coffee, and I thought he was a good guy, I would normally say yes. I think my outgoing personality and quick smile seemed to attract decent men. I didn't know how to flirt and purposely did not try. If someone told me to flirt, I might assume some cartoonish mannerisms or something. I didn't know how to consciously flirt, so I settled for being my friendly and outgoing self.

It might seem like it was a risk to my safety, and maybe it was, but I was an eternal optimist and maybe a bit naive. My cloak of protection was the "one date rule." Before my gender reassignment surgery, I would only go out on one date with the same man. There would never be a second date or anything formal. Nothing physical, it was just social. I went out for coffee, met for a drink, saw a movie, and did other activities I deemed safe. I let it be known that I was just divorced and I had no interest in more than a single date, so there was no chance of misunderstanding. To reinforce my intent, I insisted on splitting the bill anytime I went out. That threw guys off their game more than anything else.

Yet I longed for intimacy. I don't mean physical intimacy; I mean emotional intimacy. While I was desperately lonely for a deeper relationship, it didn't feel like the right time. Would someone finally love me for me, and not for who he thought I was? That was the great unknown. The big question of life: Was I lovable?

Once I had completed my gender affirmation surgery, I felt more comfortable dating. If there was a mutual attraction, I enjoyed getting to know the guy, hiking together, or just going for a long drive. I didn't have to worry if the man wanted to hug me or kiss me anymore. I felt safer since I was physically female inside my clothing. My socially outgoing soul was getting fed.

I still had a dating rule, though instead of the "one date rule," I now had a "three date rule." I figured if I liked the guy enough to make it to a third date, he must have liked my company as much as I liked his. By the third date, I think there was a mutual expectation that the quick kiss and embrace at the end of the date might lead to more. I'm not suggesting I would sleep with a guy on the third date, but the kisses might be longer, the embrace a bit more amorous.

After my divorce I was not going to get into a relationship without the man knowing full well who he was dating. My "three date rule" determined that by the end of the third date I had to tell the man about my past. So after the first date of meeting for coffee and a second date of dinner or a movie or maybe a drive in the country with a chaste kiss on the cheek, when the third date ended and we both wanted more than a quick peck on the cheek, I felt it important to be honest and spill the beans.

I found a dozen different ways to explain my past to men. To this day it makes my stomach knot up in nervous anxiety just thinking about it. It's never as simple as telling the nice man sitting next to me at dinner that, "Oh by the way, I used to be a man." Or, "I was born with some medical challenges, and it's complicated . . . I had gender surgery a few years ago." I might say "I'm transgender" and try to explain more, but I never found a way to tell a man without freaking him out. The conversations didn't get any easier no matter how many times I did it.

Sometimes I would try to keep the relationship in the platonic stage. I would wait a couple weeks between dates thinking that the lengthened time interval would dampen down the emotions and subsequent physical feelings. I think some of the guys began to think they were dating a nun.

Very few men were OK dating me once I told them about my past. That was deeply damaging to my self-esteem, and I felt horrible for the guy too. They were often hurt and confused. I can't tell you how many times I divulged my story to a nice, polite, decent man who had obviously started having feelings for me, only to have him stare back at me blankly, not understanding. The most common reply was, "But I'm not gay." It never occurred to me that guys would question their own sexual attraction when I told them of my history. "But I'm not gay." That was what I heard.

Around this time, I moved to a city of about 200,000 for a new job and a promotion. One Sunday morning after church, I met a guy while reading the paper and sipping my regular vanilla latte at the Starbucks near my home. He was sitting next to me, and we struck up a conversation.

We met up for coffee a few more times and started dating. I decided I might try to extend the "three date rule." I lied to myself and said, "Just having coffee isn't a date." And if coffee isn't a date, then meeting up to walk the trails along the river in town hardly is!

I knew Tom* would never be the love of my life, but he was a decent guy. Nice and polite and hardworking. We shared some similar interests, and I enjoyed spending time with him. One day he was having a cookout at his house and wanted me to come, so I went. I met some of his best buddies as well as his sister and mom. When I met his family, I knew I had exceeded the flexibility of my dumb "three date rule." There were reasons for the rule, even if I was the one who invented

---

* Pseudonym

it. It was past time. Tom deserved to know who he was dating before things got more serious.

I met him at a restaurant for breakfast one Sunday after church. Afterward we sat in my car, and I had the talk with him. I heard the same thing from Tom that I had heard from all the men after I told them about me.

"But I'm not gay!"

"No, I know you're not gay. I'm not either," I said, as I had many times before.

But Tom, like all the others, felt betrayed. He drove off. He was hurt and angry.

A few days later, Tom called. He wanted to talk about our conversation. He said when I told him my story, he felt like he had been punched really hard in the stomach. I had never punched anyone before. It felt horrible that I made him feel that way. He told me that he went to talk to his mom about it, and she made him feel better. She had told him, "At least Bobbie told you now before things got more serious."

It was clear: my "three date rule" had better be followed.

Even though Tom was a nice guy, and I knew we'd never be too serious, losing him was another blow to my self-esteem.

A year or so later, I moved once again for another promotion and a new job. I met a man while working out of state about three hundred miles from home. I got to see him a few times while I was working in his town. He was a friend of one of my coworkers. Joe* was definitely my type: a big, gentle man who was soft-spoken and kind. He worked in the construction business and was strong and sweet at the same time. After I went back home, he began to call me every day. I had to admit, after meeting him a couple times and sharing months of phone calls, I was falling for him. He kept asking when he could come visit. I had thought I found a way to avoid the "three date rule."

Joe was divorced and was raising his boys. The youngest was about to move out and join the military. The oldest had already gone away to college. He would be an empty nester. He began talking about moving to the town where I lived, and I thought, "OK, this is getting out of control." I was going to have to tell him.

---

* Pseudonym

In all my life, I never thought my personality was more well suited to another's. Even though we had only met a couple times, we spoke on the phone for hours every week. But I had no delusions either. By this point in my life, I had dated (meaning a date, not sex) dozens of nice men. When the "third date rule" was imposed, we usually didn't make it to the fourth date. I would have loved to get serious with Joe, but in my heart, I knew it was unlikely that he would continue to want to date me after I told him. Yet I felt I owed him honesty.

We decided to meet in a small, historical town halfway between both of our homes. It was a four-hour drive for me. When he was making reservations at the hotel, he wanted to just get one room.

"No," I told him, "separate rooms."

He was disappointed, but I knew it was important not to rush things. I brought homemade cookies for him to take home and share with his son. We went out hiking and sightseeing. It was a great day. Beautiful scenery enjoyed with a sweet man who was obviously taken with me. We walked from the hotel to the historic downtown area for dinner. It was a picturesque Old West town with two-story red brick buildings and many historical markers that we stopped to read along the way. After dinner we walked back to our hotel holding hands and enjoying each other's company like an old comfortable couple. I was trying to ignore what was likely to happen in the next hour.

When we got to my room, we walked in and sat down. He looked intently at me and said, "OK, I want to know why you're keeping your emotional distance from me. Why aren't you letting me in?"

My heart sank. I was amazed that this tough but sweet construction worker was so acutely aware of my feelings. I knew this was it.

With as much gentleness and concern as I could muster, I told him the short version of my story. He didn't ask any questions. He just sat there and looked at the floor.

Finally, he said, "But I'm not gay!"

There it was.

"Yeah, I'm not gay either," I said.

Joe got up and ran his hand through his hair while he walked around the room.

"I've got to go outside. I need some fresh air. I'll talk to you in the morning."

I cried myself to sleep that night because of all the men I had dated, I thought Joe could be the man who would be openhearted enough to love the whole person I was. And I also knew it wasn't going to work out. Because things don't really work out; life doesn't have fairy-tale endings.

In the morning, the dish of cookies and a note sat in the hallway at my door. The note simply said, "I can't do this."

Of all the men I'd lost and would lose in the future, I think my heart broke the most over Joe. I cried the entire four-hour drive home and for many years to come. Losing Joe was one of those significant emotional events that would stand out in my life. And I had many of them. But losing Joe hurt more than I thought it should.

On the drive home I thought, *Well, maybe my brother is right.*

Years before, one of my brothers told me, "No man will ever love you."

At the time, I truly believed he was wrong. But I thought he was wrong because guys seemed to like me. How could he think that about me? I mean, guys were always asking me out. At the time, I hadn't yet lost dozens of nice, polite, good, and decent men. I never considered another possibility.

Now I started thinking that maybe my brother was right. I hated that he might be right, not only because he's my brother, but also because it was such a deliberately cruel thing to say to me.

We all learn to avoid hurt in our lives. I learned that if I broke up with a guy before I had to tell him about my past, it didn't hurt quite as much. I could always find a reason to break up that saved me having to have the talk with him. There were lots of options. None of them were great, but they afforded me an escape without being rejected.

If my romantic life was a depressing bust, my social network of friends was my blessing. I felt truly lucky, fortunate, blessed. Every place I moved to for my job, I developed a great network of women friends. There were even a few men who became the caring big brothers I never had.

I knew if I was going to have real long-lasting meaningful relationships with my women friends, I had to tell them who I was. There are
some I've talked to in the transgender community who believe that if I
could "pass," why tell anyone? Why tell a man you're dating? Why tell
your women friends? If they don't know anything, why would you tell
them? The answer to that question is simple. I will not lie to someone
I'm close to. I never felt like I needed to tell the world about who I
was or what I had gone through, but I couldn't swap one set of lies for
another. I couldn't consider such a thing. If someone liked me, they
were going to know who they liked. That went even more so for a
romantic relationship.

I learned that I could tell close friends about my past, and it never
was a problem. It generated lots of questions and long discussions, but
no woman ever ended a friendship with me when she learned about
my past. Guys who were just friends and learned my history also stayed
friends with me. But men who had romantic feelings for me were different. Few stayed around too long after we had the talk.

Eventually, I entered into a long-term relationship with a nice man.
He seemed unfazed by my third-date declaration. I was crying as I told
him about being transgender. I cried because I had been down this road
so many times before and I knew the ultimate outcome.

But he didn't seem concerned. Instead of reiterating the familiar
comment that I had heard so many times, "But I'm not gay," he said,
"Just tell me you're not married." That was his concern. No, I wasn't
married.

Lies come in ways you don't anticipate, though, building up over
time through hundreds of moments of omission. Over the years, I
became close to his family. I was a part of their holiday celebrations and
family events like weddings. Joining in, I felt like a part of a big family
again. I hadn't been a part of my family in more than fifteen years, and
I missed it so much. I finally had a sense of belonging to a family again.

But I couldn't feel fully accepted because I couldn't be honest about
who I was. My boyfriend insisted that no one know my history. Like in
my marriage, where I couldn't talk with anyone about my struggles, with
my new partner and extended family, once again, I couldn't be honest

about who I was. The irony was amazing. In my life I went from being a male hiding my true gender identity to being female but unable to share who I was and what I had been through.

It made me uncomfortable and anxious. What if I slipped up? What if I said something incriminating? What if my stories didn't line up? When you lie, you'd better be good at it. I learned to be good at not sharing, not at lying.

When one of his family members was talking about an upcoming wedding, everyone would share the details of their wedding. I couldn't share. Someone would say, "What style of dress did you wear?" All I could do was change the subject or pretend I didn't hear. When the subject came around to having kids, and they all knew I had two adult children and four grandkids, invariably the conversation included being pregnant, labor, and childbirth. Again, I'd have to leave the room to go fill my glass of water or use the bathroom. I could never share with his family that I couldn't attend my children's graduations or their wedding celebrations or my grandchildren's birthdays and on and on and on. It's an unbalanced kind of a relationship when others are sharing about themselves, and you're not allowed to.

Dishonesty comes in degrees. I never felt I was dishonest to act and look like any other woman. It's who I was, who I am. But it's a slippery slope. Most times, I didn't feel like it would have made any sense to wave a flag and announce, "I'm transgender!" It didn't make sense because my gender struggles weren't a part of the conversation, and I thought most people just didn't want to know.

I never felt the need to tell everyone I knew my story. But when friends become closer, in order to develop emotional intimacy, they start sharing things about their divorce, their children, dysfunctional families, and other important milestones and events in their life. Like all close friends, I learned of my friend's sexual abuse as a child, a divorce because of a cheating husband, some deep-seated crippling insecurities, and all the other things that are real in all our lives. It was only normal that I would share my own heartache. Usually with a bottle of wine being shared with friends, I'd share my story too. Because at some point, you need to be honest. When a relationship hits that tipping point, you either tell a lie, you lie by omission, or you let them in to your world. I have to be honest. It's who I am.

My high school years were a mixture of confusion and accomplishment. Looking back at those years, the dichotomy was huge. In some ways, I loved being in high school. I had some great times and developed friendships that would last for a lifetime. But in other ways, those days were so painful. I came through it alive, which is more than what happens to many transgender teens.

My high school was a unique environment. It was a Catholic school with about 650 students. Within the rare environment, the class of '73 was even more exceptional. We had a genuine appreciation for the school and our class. But let's be honest, when you're seventeen years old, you don't know exactly what you have. It was in the following years that I think we all began to appreciate just what we had and how special our high school years were.

I attended my ten-year reunion. I was still married and firmly stuck in the male role I had been playing. By my twenty-year reunion, my fabric covering was battered and torn, and I was in no emotional state to go. Ten years later I was fully female, having transitioned years before, but I remained in the dark shadow of family-imposed guilt. My parents still saw many of my high school friends' parents at church. My parents had only minimal communication with me, and I knew I was a huge embarrassment to them. So I stayed away to avoid creating any awkwardness for them. I was like the kid that was kept in the basement so the neighbors didn't know. The only difference was I kept myself in my own basement. When I was home with my friends and succeeding at work, I was just fine. But when it came to my family, I allowed myself to be put into the role of the outcast. And I assumed the role quite well.

As much as I wanted to go to the thirty-year reunion, I stayed away. Staying away from my friends reinforced my shame. But now it was self-inflicted shame. I was forty-eight years old and still worried about what my parents would say. I'm embarrassed by that now.

Our graduating class didn't like to have to wait decades between get-togethers. Everyone wanted to see each other more often, so a small group of classmates began having yearly reunions. By the thirty-first reunion, I decided enough was enough. I traveled to Arizona to reconnect with my friends. I still had a friend or two whom I communicated with, and many in the class already knew about my big change, but I'll always remember standing out in the parking lot of a neighborhood bar. I could see through the fence into the outside seating area of the bar. It was a great space under big eucalyptus trees with small bonfires burning with chairs gathered around the fires. As I stood away from the light of the fires and old friends, I could see the familiar faces of the jocks as they stood around the campfire. I hadn't seen them since the tenth reunion. These were the guys I was most concerned about seeing. I put the jocks into the category of "people who won't be accepting of Bobbie."

I walked up to the group of guys and said, "Hey, I'm looking for the reunion."

They stared at me. "Do you know someone from our class?"

"Yeah," I said. "I'm Bobbie Scopa."

Instantly they were on their feet and giving me hugs.

"Oh my gosh! How come you've stayed away so long? We're so glad you're here!"

The guys I was most concerned about meeting were so welcoming I almost burst into tears. Truthfully, I waited until I got back to my hotel, and then I did cry. How sweet could I have hoped the jocks would be? They turned out to be amazing. Now, every year when I see them, we exchange hugs, and I add them to my list of things to be grateful for.

As our other classmates trickled in, the jocks made a point to introduce me to our classmates. The jocks were trying to make sure my reintroduction into the class was easy for me. I'm rather outgoing, so I didn't really need the introductions, but I loved that they wanted to make sure I was included. By the end of the evening, it was like I had never been away from my wonderful classmates.

Old friendships picked up where we left them so many years before. Those old friendships blossomed into new friendships that went beyond anything that I had with my friends years before.

How can that be? Why is it? Is it because we're older now and we can see the important things in life better than we could when we were younger and consumed with careers and raising families? Maybe we're closer now because I can be honest, and they know the real me. I don't profess to know why. But I'm so incredibly thankful for my family of friends now.

After my divorce, my parents quit talking to me. I was specifically told not to attend the large family gatherings at their home. They wanted nothing to do with me. From their perspective, the divorce was all my fault. From their perspective, I had abandoned my children. They were unable to see the pain I endured for so many years. They didn't care that I didn't want the divorce and didn't want to leave my children. In their mind the solution was easy: I should just cut my hair, buck up, and be a man. Those expectations were so far out of my reach. I could not be the man they wanted me to be; I could not pretend any longer.

I knew my parents loved me. They loved me the only way they knew how. It wasn't love in the way I tend to think about it, but it was love in their own style. I felt sorry for them because I knew they were hurting for my children and for themselves. I began writing and sending them letters two or three times a month. I described what I was doing at work and with my friends. Sometimes I sent pictures of where I was working, places I knew they would be interested in. It was my way of staying in touch and trying to maintain some relationship.

I never heard back.

When I came back from New York City following my work at the World Trade Center and all had I experienced there, it became crystal clear to me what was important in life. I thought it was important for my parents to reconnect with me. I knew their lives would be in turmoil and filled with fear and anxiety if they couldn't have a relationship with me. I feared for their emotional health. Up until the last few years we had been so close—and now they wouldn't even talk to me. I tried to encourage them to talk to me. I reminded them that "as we get older, we should be pulling closer together, not pulling apart." My words were ignored. They didn't want any part of me.

My son's wedding had been planned for some time, but due to my mom's failing health, she wouldn't be able to travel the thousand miles cross-country to attend. My considerate son and his wonderful bride decided to have the wedding ceremony out west, where my parents lived. Their reception would take place later, back east as they'd planned.

This was my chance to attend at least one of my children's life events. I had missed all their previous high school and college graduations, birthdays, my daughter's wedding, and the birth of a grandchild. I was never invited due to the strained relationships and family dynamics. But this wedding was different. It would take place in my hometown, and none of my ex-wife's friends would be there. It would be attended by just a few of my parents' friends. I asked if I could come and was told that, yes, I could attend the wedding—on one condition.

My mom insisted that I had to come dressed as a man.

It had been eight years since I had tried to dress and pass as a man. I was dumbstruck. What would that even look like? In shock, I agreed. If that's what it was going to take to attend my son's wedding, I would swallow my pride and dress up as a man.

I wore a pair of black slacks and a men's button-down dress shirt. My hair was in a ponytail. I was doing my best impression of a man I could muster. It was a waste of effort. Regardless of how I was dressed, anyone who didn't know me addressed me as ma'am. My mom's friends asked who I was. When I told them who my mom and dad were, they looked confused.

"We didn't think they had another daughter."

I smiled sadly and walked away.

When the wedding day arrived, my mom was in the hospital and couldn't attend after all, so I visited her afterward. I didn't know how serious her illness was, but I wasn't going to miss this opportunity to see her. If she wanted to kick me out of her room, she could, but I was going to make the effort to try and connect with her.

When I walked into the hospital room she shared with another patient, the other patient and visitors were walking out of the room. Before I could even say hi to my mom, a teenage girl visiting the other patient pointed at me and said, "Look, Mom, that lady looks just like Aunt Rose." I just smiled at her as they walked out of the room.

I asked my mom how she was feeling and all the normal pleasantries that you'd ask any acquaintance you're visiting in the hospital. My mom didn't waste much time, though. She quickly started scolding me for breaking apart my family.

"What kind of a father are you?"

"How dare you break your family's heart."

"You should be ashamed of yourself."

For years I tried to be kind and understanding. For years I had reached out over and over again, trying to talk to them. Wanting to see them. But this latest admonishment was more than I could handle. I had spent the day being humiliated, dressed up pretending to be a man. After all these years, that day I felt like I had lost all my hard-fought self-esteem.

"Mom, how dare me? How dare you! Where were you when you knew I was struggling? Where were you when I was kicked out of my home? Where were you when I couldn't see my children anymore? Where were you when your child was confused and ashamed and didn't know where to turn? How dare you, Mom, how dare you!"

Years of pent-up frustration and hurt came out in a few seconds.

It didn't last long. My diatribe was over. I stood next to her bed and didn't say anything. I didn't want this to be our last conversation, but I didn't know what else to do anymore. I had tried and tried for so long, and it came to this. She was dying, and now I was scolding her.

She responded, "All I need is a week or two at home after I have surgery. I'll cook for a few days and fill the freezer for your dad, so he has meals to last him for a while. Then I'll come up north and stay with you for a few weeks."

She was going to come stay with me? After all these years, she said she was going to come visit and stay with me. That was as close to an apology I would ever get. And actually, it was quite good.

Before I left her hospital room, she looked up at me and said, "You have to be the *nani* now."

My mom was dying, and she had passed the torch to me. It warmed my heart, but it was too little, too late for our family. The die had been cast. The examples were set. No one knew I had been given the torch from my mom.

Less than a week later I was back home when I got a call from a family member. My mom had her surgery. It was an inoperable tumor. She was now in hospice with only a few days left. If I wanted to see her before she was gone, I should get down to Phoenix quickly. I jumped in my little yellow VW Beetle and headed south.

When I arrived, she was on palliative care. She couldn't talk. She tried but had no breath left in her. She would actually stand up with the help of my daughter and niece and pretend she was doing a jig. Her sense of humor was alive even while she was dying. I stood by her bed holding her hand, talking to her.

"I love you, Mom."

She tried to respond but couldn't.

"It's OK, Mom, I know you love me. It's OK, don't talk. I know you love me."

In my heart I knew she was trying to talk, so she could apologize or at least say she loved me. But it was too late. She couldn't get the words out.

Later during the night, she passed away.

A few family members and I were in the room with my dad when my mom took her last breath. That scene probably took place a dozen times a day in that hospice facility, but it felt unique to us. My dad held her hand for at least thirty minutes after she passed, while I stood next to him alongside the bed.

Finally, he took ahold of my hand while still holding my mom's hand, looked at me, and said, "Please forgive me for what's happened."

We had a few years left together before my dad passed away at ninety-five, and for that I feel we were both blessed. But I can't help but feel so many years were wasted. Years when both my parents would have benefited from having their loving child with them. Emotions wasted on the fear, the shame of what people might think. Anger over what "I had done to them."

In the end, what did any of that matter? How many of us were hurt, how many lives left lonely and wanting because of a fear of what might have been, what others would say or think? It was hardly worth the distance it created between us, and all it did was delay the inevitable.

Somehow, somewhere deep inside of me I always knew I was going to be who I was. It took me decades to consciously choose that, but I must have always known, and decades too late they would realize it too. I was always their daughter. I had and would always love them. I wish it hadn't taken them so long to see that.

When I get sad about the loss of my family, I remind myself that I have family. They are my chosen family: my friends, including those from high school that I still love and appreciate every day. In many ways, I'm one of the most fortunate people I know.

When I'm gone for the summer up in the cool waters of Washington's Puget Sound, I communicate weekly with my friends in Phoenix. I miss them all summer. And when I'm in the Phoenix area for the winter, I call and talk to my friends in the northwest. I always have friends nearby. How blessed can a person be?

14

LOOKING AHEAD

IT'S A CHILLY MORNING. I pull back the covers and get out of bed. I put on a sweatshirt to warm up, climb up the stairs to the galley, and turn on the coffee maker. I look out the windows to make sure that my anchor held firm all through the night. My Nordic Tug thirty-two-foot boat named *Florian*, after Saint Florian, who is the patron saint of firefighters, is my home for six months out of each year. I look out the windows at the island I'm anchored beside. The tall, dark-green fir trees come all the way down the steep hillside of the island to the rocky shore.

I walk outside onto the deck to enjoy the cool morning. This scene is something I have dreamt of since I was twenty years old. The beauty of the Puget Sound, the hundreds of islands, the whales, the snowcapped peaks surrounding the water. By chance, through hard work and with many blessings, here I am. The sun hasn't yet evaporated all the morning dew on the deck. Everything is still wet, so I go back inside my cozy cabin to make some muffins while my coffee brews.

In a few days, I will head back to the marina where I keep *Florian* moored. A retired firefighter friend of mine will meet me there. We'll go out for a couple days to do some exploring of the islands. Maybe we'll head down toward Seattle or north into Canada. I haven't decided yet. In the meantime, I'll have time to enjoy the scenery while at anchor, relax, put out a crab pot, read a book, enjoy some music, and think about the stories from my life—and those not yet lived.

I take my big mug of hot coffee with a hot muffin fresh from the oven up to the top deck. I unfold one of the chairs and tables and watch the activities on the other boats moored around the little island. Paddleboarders and kayakers slowly make their way around the island, navigating through the other boats. The ones who come close by always get a wave and an invitation for a cup of coffee. If half of them ever took me up on my offer of hospitality, I'd have to start bringing a lot more coffee. But the invite usually starts a little pleasant conversation about where the paddlers are from and what boat they're staying on.

As a retirement plan goes, spending my summers on the Puget Sound with the occasional trip to British Columbia and Alaska isn't a bad one. Winters are spent back home in Arizona, where I can enjoy the beauty of the desert while escaping the cold and wet of the northwest winters. This situation allows me a certain amount of adventure that I still have a need for after forty-five years in the fire service. I don't need or want a lot of excitement. Boating can deliver too much adventure if you're not careful, but I love a little bit. It also gives me time to think. I think about everything I still want to do, but I also think about my children, grandchildren, and the life I've already lived.

When any of us are raising kids, our life revolves around them. We help them with their schoolwork. We try to comfort them and dry their tears. We worry about and deal with our own anxiety, tailoring our lives in order for them to be healthy and happy. It's all consuming. How can it not be?

Work consumes us as well. We worry about what our boss thinks. We worry about a coworker who may be trying to make us look bad. We wonder if we have a chance at that next promotion. We get anxious when the boss puts unrealistic expectations on us. The list goes on.

Being immersed in the day-to-day can leave little time to think about life's personal challenges—the large and the seemingly small. Every-thing else becomes secondary. My life has been no different, even if my personal life presented more complications than most. I kept my head down and just worked.

Now, sitting at anchor, enjoying the beauty of nature, sipping my coffee, and eating my muffin, I have time to think, time to contemplate what's next and to think about all that's gone before. That's a big thing to think about. What's next after a significant career? To look back and evaluate what I did, and what I should have done differently, can be pretty scary. But it's only scary if you're honest with yourself.

Regrets? Yeah, as Sinatra sang, I've had a few. A few thousand, maybe. I should have fought to stay in my children's lives. That's my biggest regret and failing. But of course, I have others. I believe we should all be honest and acknowledge our mistakes and where we could have done better. That's the only way we improve. It's the way we grow to be better human beings.

As I sit and enjoy the view from the upper deck of *Florian*, I think about my career. My last seven years were spent working at the regional office of the US Forest Service in Portland, Oregon. I was the assistant fire director for all wildland fire operations in Oregon, Washington, and Alaska for the US Forest Service. I even spent six months filling in as the deputy fire director for fire operations in Washington, DC. How did I go from struggling in my career to holding one of the highest fire positions in wildland fire in the country?

I rarely sought out the promotions. I was fortunate that on several occasions I was even recruited for multiple jobs at the same time. It was ironic because my career ambition had never been that important to me. What I always wanted was to live a low-key, ordinary life with a little home and family snug inside. My vision was the modest home with a white-picket fence and smoke coming out of the chimney, with children playing in the yard. I kind of lived that image for a short time when I was married, and maybe again when I put up a picket fence around a home all my own. But ultimately, that wasn't how my life turned out. What happened?

What I really wanted, what I had hoped and prayed for after my divorce, was to eventually meet a nice guy who could accept the whole of me and marry him. I would have loved settling down somewhere, my job becoming secondary to my relationship. But I never had the relationship, so my career and friends filled my life.

Prior to my transition, I was successful in my career—but it was always a lot of work to make things happen. At the fire department, despite being promoted early and quickly, I never felt truly successful. In order to achieve my accomplishments, I felt like I was constantly swimming upstream, against the current. They were hard-fought struggles because I was always trying to prove myself worthy. More important, I never felt like I belonged. I chose the fire service because of the cover I thought it would provide me, and though I grew into it and loved it, I never felt welcomed by most of my fellow firefighters, even if I was a leader in the organization.

Every success felt tainted. I remember on more than one occasion a supervisor announcing, "Well, I have to give the job to Scopa," as if he didn't want to give me a promotion I deserved and knew my coworkers wouldn't be happy about it. My career had been successful in spite of my employers and supervisors, and probably in spite of my own insecurities and failings. I had proved myself through testing and performance.

After I transitioned, my career blossomed. Promotions presented themselves to me when I wasn't even looking for them. I was asked to apply for positions that in the past I would have never been considered for. The cynic in me would say that since I was female, I received job offers because an employer was looking to fill a position with a diverse candidate. I actually pulled my job application once when I found out the employer specifically wanted a woman for the job. If I couldn't get the job on my own merits, I didn't want it. In fact, I was quite confident in my ability to outcompete most of the men I was up against. I had the education, the experience, and the technical fire qualifications. But there was more to it than simple credentials.

Why was I so much more successful in my career as a woman than as a man? And not just any career, but a career in a male-dominated field like firefighting?

There is no definitive answer, and I believe like most issues the easy answer is too simplistic, not nuanced enough to really address the complexities of the discussion.

Could it be as simple as the emphasis in diversity hiring within the federal government? That's what many men I know would say: "You're getting promoted because you're a female." Those would be their exact words. They would say that the reason they haven't gotten promoted is because they're White men and White men can't get promoted anymore. But had they worked for multiple fire agencies gaining valuable experience along the way like I had? Did they have multiple degrees relating to their job? Did they have a track record of successes in their career? I can't answer for all of them, but I believe many men were so used to getting promoted as a matter of course, that when it wasn't happening as automatically for them anymore, they had to blame someone else and not take responsibility for improving their own competitiveness as a candidate.

To present an honest picture of diversity within the federal wildland fire agencies, I am personally aware of many young women who have been run off from the federal fire agencies including the US Forest Service, the Bureau of Land Management, and the National Park Service. These young, smart, strong women would be assets to their agencies, but were harassed to the point of being forced to quit their job. I watched it. I tried to stop it, but no matter how hard I tried, I couldn't. In fact, one reason I retired when I did was due to my own case of discrimination. The Bureau of Land Management conducted no real investigation into my claims of sexual discrimination. Witnesses told me very directly that they were afraid of retribution if they spoke up, so they did not. Even though the agency knew the supervisor had a history of problems, they refused to deal with him. In an office where there had been seven women working, by the time I left, there was only one. It's hard for me to have much sympathy for the guys complaining about the agencies trying to hire more women.

When the public reads the paper and sees that a city has hired a female police or fire chief, the response is typically, "Oh, look at the progress, they hired a woman." But it's easy for a city council to hire a female fire chief—or for the secretary of agriculture to hire a woman for the role of US Forest Service chief. The real question is: How are women and other diverse employees down in the ranks being treated by their coworkers, captains, and battalion chiefs? That's the real measure of an organization. Not who the politicians are hiring. In recent years, it would appear that the Forest Service has promoted more women to the executive ranks than men. From the outside the public rallies, "Oh look, they hired a female director or female chief. It's such great progress." All the while the women in the lower ranks are being run off.

The disparity between hiring diversity at the highest levels of the agency and the treatment of women and diverse candidates in the middle or lower portions of the agency is seriously flawed. When I retired in 2018, the only actions being taken were talk and hand-wringing. Nothing more. Maybe it's better now. Maybe things have greatly improved. Maybe.

But probably not.

Looking back, I can see now that my confidence levels soared after my transition and surgery. It must have been obvious to my supervisors and coworkers too. I believe that my self-confidence and comfort in who I was helped me become successful. Think about that. What about other people like me who never get to transition? How would their lives be different if they could transition too? The pressures that we put on our children's shoulders because we want them to act like people they're not—in any sense—can be overwhelming.

In the 1980s I wasn't even considered for an entry-level fire manager position. But in 2017, I spent six months detailed to the national headquarters of the US Forest Service in Washington, DC, as the deputy fire director. Times had changed. Was it me or was it them?

I believe it was a combination of factors that improved my career trajectory. Being a woman might have helped at times, but I know it hurt at times too. As my experience and education increased, I looked better to future employers. But the biggest factor, that I believe made the difference, was how I had changed. I was more self-assured now. I didn't worry about what people were saying about me. Oh, there was probably just as much talk about me as before, only now I didn't care because I was truly being me and not pretending anymore. And, more important in my opinion, a male-dominated field like firefighting can deal with a strong, competent female firefighter much better than they can deal with what they perceive as a competent but "feminine" male firefighter.

As I sit on my boat, enjoying this personal peace I've created, I often think of all the transgender people in the world. I think about their parents, their siblings, wives and husbands, employers, coworkers, and family friends. I'm sixty-seven years old now. I'm retired. What do I have to be afraid of?

For years I kept my head down and just worked. When living as a male, I never acknowledged my personal gender struggles. For the last twenty-five years I couldn't or wouldn't tell too many people my story. Could I have been a positive force if I had been more open about who I was? My own insecurities and fear of losing my job kept me quiet. I just wanted to be known for being a good firefighter, a good fire chief, a good leader. I didn't want to muddy the waters with discussions of being transgender. I was anxious about my employees and coworkers knowing about me—even if in reality, they probably already did. Fear drives irrational behavior. But I don't have to worry now. My career as a fire chief and fire leader have changed. It's not over; it's just different. Now I can provide leadership in a different way.

If a transgender person's boss, friend, spouse, or parent is understanding of their employee or loved one, it could make all the difference in their lives. If one of those lost souls who sat in the group therapy sessions with me had had a loving and understanding boss, family member, or friend, would their lives have taken a different course? I think so. It takes so much energy to live in the reality of being transgender.

But it doesn't have to.

There's a ripple effect from our language, our behavior, and our conduct. When someone is fired for being transgender, or spoken poorly about, those around that conversation, not just the person being talked about, are affected by the language. It's the same whether it's sexual harassment or racist gossip. We're all connected by invisible threads. When someone is mistreated, ignored, or minimized, their life is directly affected. As their life is affected in a negative way, those invisible threads radiate out to those around them. My family, friends, and coworkers were all touched by what I went through. Some of those effects were obvious and direct, but some weren't. Grown children, friends, and family are still affected many years later by what happened to me.

Dysfunctional families don't have a patent on destructive behavior. Work organizations can be pretty dysfunctional as well. Dysfunctionality in the workplace can lead to poor performance and unrelated disruptions for that organization. How an employee is treated at work impacts them beyond the organization, following them home to their children and spouse. We're all connected.

I didn't speak up years ago when my good friend made fun of a transgender person in front of me and our coworkers. It might have seemed like an innocent joke to those present, but no one spoke up and said anything. All I could do was make a pathetic comment that "none of us know what's going on in people's lives." One negative comment ripples through the threads to each of us. Maybe it's subtle, but the effect is real and lasting. We hear a comment, no one refutes it, and now it's considered OK to make a similar comment ourselves.

The only knowledge some people have of transgender people is what they see on TV or in news programs. A celebrity comes out as trans, and almost immediately the negative comments fly about on social media, like snow in a mountain blizzard. Others jump to stubbornly defend them. I have to confess my own fatigue with celebrities coming out. None of them seem ordinary to me. Who can identify with a celebrity?

I don't feel like I have anything in common with a celebrity coming out as transgender. I couldn't afford cosmetic surgery to make me beautiful or voluptuous. I didn't have makeup artists available to do my makeup for the cameras. Clothes? Who has the money to spend on designer outfits? Like most ordinary people, I did my clothes shopping at the local department stores, for when I wasn't wearing my firefighter uniform.

Unfortunately, we also often hear about transgender sex workers being arrested by the police or, worse, killed while working the streets. We hear far too often about transgender women, especially Black women, being murdered. That's another way the public learns about the transgender.

And since I transitioned, I've been physically assaulted twice.

The first time was while on a thirteen-hour flight back from Australia. I was returning from a three-week work trip. I was exhausted. A young man in his thirties was sitting in the middle seat next to me. I was sitting in the aisle seat. We spoke and had a nice conversation. He told me all about his young family and even showed me pictures of his wife and children. He described his business that was taking him to the United States. After dinner, the lights were turned down low so passengers could sleep more comfortably. I was watching a movie with my headphones on. The man pulled a blanket over his lap, and I assumed he was going to drift off to sleep. But after a few minutes his hand crept out from his blanket and began to push between my legs. I was dumbfounded.

I looked at him and said, "What are you doing?" I picked up his hand and put it back in his lap.

He smiled at me and started touching me again.

"No, stop it!"

I was amazed at his brazenness. Again, I picked up his hand and this time forcefully pushed it down onto his lap. He just smiled impishly, closed his eyes, and pulled his blanket up like he was a child going to sleep again.

What was I supposed to do? I couldn't sit there for another ten hours next to someone who had put his hand between my legs trying to fondle me. I got up and started walking around the darkened jetliner looking for another seat. There wasn't one empty seat that I could find.

I was too embarrassed to tell a flight attendant. What would I say? A cute young guy was trying to touch me? I was an overweight, fifty-something-year-old woman. Who would believe me? Would the flight attendants cause a scene? He would deny it, and I would be embarrassed and look foolish. I spent the next 10 hours walking around the plane, trying to stand next to the emergency exits to get a glimpse of the ocean 40,000 feet below. I was miserable.

Another time, an ex-boyfriend of one of my good friends was driving through the town where I lived. He was always a nice guy who had been helpful to me when they lived nearby, and I had been sad to learn of their breakup. So when he told me he would be driving through my city, I invited him to use my spare bedroom rather than getting a hotel for the night.

When he got to my place at the end of his long drive, we went out for dinner at one of the nearby neighborhood restaurants. We each had a beer or two, and it had been a pleasant evening so far. When we got back to my home, we sat down in the living room to keep talking. He sat down on the couch, so I purposely sat in the big easy chair to keep my distance, not wanting to give him the wrong impression.

While we were sitting there talking, he said, "Oh, there's something I always wanted to do."

He got up from the couch abruptly. I thought he was going to get something from the bedroom or go to the bathroom. Instead, he walked over to me in the big chair, leaned down, and put his full weight on top of me and started kissing me.

"No, no, stop!" I shouted at him. He raised himself up off me and smiled.

"Go sit down," I said firmly.

He had his hands on either side of my shoulders on the easy chair with his face inches from mine.

"What are you doing, John?* No, go sit down."

I thought he was finished, but he was not. Instead, he leaned down and started forcefully kissing me and pushing himself on top of me.

I always had this idea that I was fairly strong and tough—and I was. But I wasn't strong or tough enough. My hands were on his shoulders and arms, and I was trying to push him off me. I couldn't move him. All I could feel were muscles. In that moment I knew I was in trouble.

He kept kissing me and forcing himself on top of me. There was no way I could push him off me. I felt a flash of fear.

I kept repeating, "No, John, no," while trying to push him away.

Finally, he stopped. I jumped up and off that big easy chair and looked at him.

"It's time for you to go to bed. I'm going to my room, and you go to your room, John."

I walked down the hallway to my bedroom shaking and scared. I tried to lock my bedroom door, but the lock wouldn't work. I had never tried locking the door before, and when I needed it, it didn't work. I was too afraid to sleep in my bed. I went into my large walk-in closet and made a bed on the floor. I hoped that way, if he snuck into my bedroom, he wouldn't find me.

---

* Pseudonym

Why hadn't I just kicked him out of my home? Why did I let him spend the night? I don't know. I was afraid of him and afraid to tell anyone. But the next morning at the office, I told one of my best friends and coworkers. She treated the incident like it was an assault and me like the victim. I was shaken to my core.

People I know have said to me, "At least you haven't had to deal with men's sexual harassment or assault." Every time I hear a phrase like that, my mind wanders back to the hotshot crew where my coworker kept on about my "fine ass." I incredulously think about the young man on the plane coming back from Australia putting his hands in my crotch. I fearfully remember the guy who I thought was my friend, forcing his whole body on top of mine to kiss me and who knows what else.

Someone close to me once said, "Well, you knew what you were getting into when you chose to be a woman."

Those were hurtful words. They assumed my gender was a choice.

The words also assumed that sexual assault was just a part of being a woman. It shouldn't be.

How many people work with a transgender person? How many people have a family member, a close friend, or a neighbor who's transgender? You might know several; you just don't know it yet. Maybe they've transitioned already. Maybe they haven't or never will. Maybe they're struggling within their own minds. We're having lunch with you. We're sitting next to you in church. We're who you share an office with. Maybe we look a bit different. Maybe we don't. But we're there next to you. Believe me.

For much of my life, I've lived in small rural communities. They're where I feel the most at home. And I think it's those smaller communities that have the least exposure to transgender people. In my experience, people living in small rural communities tend to think of transgender people as a big city thing. It isn't, of course. Maybe some transgender people gravitate to the big city where they can live more anonymously without the scorn and ridicule of their neighbors, but there have long been and still are many transgender people living in small towns. I know I wasn't the only one.

I've had much to be thankful for in my life. I grew up in a stable home. I had opportunities to get an education, which meant I'd had a better chance for employment. And I believe being five-foot-six and looking reasonably feminine allowed me to have a relatively "normal" life throughout the process of transitioning.

Perhaps I'm more accepted now because I look like an "ordinary woman" and not like the horrible phrase I've heard so often: "a man in a dress." What about those souls who don't look on the outside like they feel on the inside? How do we treat them? Why do we treat them—or allow others to treat them—with disdain and withhold acceptance? Why can't we let people be who they are?

It breaks my heart to think about another child having to feel that they are the result of a science experiment gone awry like I did. Those little children who already know who they are at five or six or seven years old, who feel alone in trying to understand or convey their gender identity to those around them. They need to be listened to. I pray that parents take their children to knowledgeable gender therapists. Listen to the professionals. Please don't try to force your children to play a role that isn't their authentic selves. They might not push back against your wishes, but they will eventually have to deal with their gender identity issues, and the path they take could be one of immense struggle, even life ending. We all have a role to play in supporting our children and our friends in our lives.

I'm an expert on me. And that's all. I'm not an expert on all transgender people. I can't speak for others. Everyone's reality is different. Just like no two redheaded guys from Philadelphia have the same life experiences, the same is true for everyone else. Just because a transgender person has different experiences and feelings than me or you, it doesn't make their life and opinions any more or less valid.

Everyone alive is born into a distinct role or position. You might be the oldest sibling in a large family. Perhaps you were born into poverty or grew up with emotionally distant parents. Some people are born with medical problems and have to deal with a lifetime of hospital stays and invasive surgeries and treatments. No one has the perfect life.

Some of the "perfect" families I knew growing up had their own issues. When I got older, I learned of alcoholism and drug abuse, sexual molestations, gambling addictions, moms and dads having affairs, and the list goes on. My family friends thought that my ex-wife and I had the perfect marriage. That was their view from the street looking in through our living room window.

In my case, I had to deal with my gender dysphoria. It wasn't the worst problem to have, but it changed my life and the lives of all my loved ones. Due to the era I grew up in, my family and I made it worse than it had to be. Looking back now, I see how we all failed ourselves and each other. But that's what we do: we fail and then we pick ourselves up and try to move on. We will all fail. It's the human condition. We cannot always be right. But my hope is that when we fail, we fail with love around us. When we fail, we need to reach out to each other and try to do better. We have to do better in love.

I began to become aware of what's important in life after my sister's death in 1977. Then because of my work, I became acutely aware of what was important in life on nearly every shift. Through all the death I've witnessed and the terror those who died and those who loved them experienced and continue to grapple with, there is one enduring truth: everything I believe to be important at the end of our lives is not just how we lived—it's how we loved.

What kind of a job we have, how much money we make, the size of our home . . . it's all irrelevant. What is important is how we love and are loved. Love is an action verb. It *requires* action. Love can't be just a word we use to describe how we feel about someone. This became paramount in my life when I was ostracized by some friends and family. They would say, "Oh, I love you, but you've done this terrible thing to the family." How is that love?

If we fully loved ourselves, loving others would be easier. When any of us are having difficulty loving ourselves, loving others becomes impossible. Our world would be such a better place if we all took a leadership role in love, in caring. Take action.

Where will my adventures take me on *Florian*? I don't know. But I won't be alone. I'll be going with friends. And I hope and pray that someday I'll be able to spend more time exploring the desert mountains of Arizona and the islands of the Pacific Northwest with my children and grandchildren. We may not be close, but they caught the love of the outdoors from me, and it is a shared connection that I cherish.

My children exceeded any expectations that I had for their success in life. They both have advanced graduate degrees. One has a PhD and is teaching. I'm so thankful for their successes. As I watch their lives from a distance, I see how they are as parents. I've watched them set expectations for and communicate with their own children in calm, loving ways. I hear about their family adventures on boats, rock climbing, and camping. It sounds like a great, loving life.

When I do get to see them, my heart always swells with pride for the incredible people they have become. But it also breaks with longing: to be recognized as their parent and as a grandparent to their children. I yearn for that familial bond, that loving relationship we shared decades ago, when we were all growing up, growing into who we would become. I remind myself that, in the big picture of life, I know I am a part of their success. I contributed to who they are today whether they recognize it or not. That has to be enough for me.

My dream of having an ordinary life with the white-picket fence was just that, a dream. I really thought eventually I would have my family and grandchildren around me as I grew old. It hurts to admit that my dreams were just that. But I'm OK. I'll be just fine. I'm soundly anchored, like *Florian* beneath me.

I am anchored by my values: love, kindness, and decency. My summer months spent encompassed by the glacier-tipped mountain peaks and fir-covered islands keep me connected to my faith and the gift of the Holy Spirit. The beauty surrounding me is my reminder of all the gifts I've been given. I will experience my adventures with loving friends along the way, all the while holding hope for a reunion with my family. I continue to have hope for the future. Anything less than hope seems ungrateful in light of all the blessings I know I've received. After all, what could be better than hope?